SUCCESS PATHS BUSINESS SERIES

How to Start and Run a Successful Small Business

Ted Clifton

How to Start and Run a Successful Small Business
Ted Clifton
Paperback edition 978-1-77342-116-2
Ebook edition 978-1-77342-115-5

Published by PurpleSage Books LLC
www.TedClifton.com

Produced by IndieBookLauncher.com
www.IndieBookLauncher.com
Cover Design: Saul Bottcher
Interior Design and Typesetting: Saul Bottcher

The body text of this book is set in Adobe Caslon.

Contents

Starting a New Business

1

Working for Yourself?

This book is a conversation between you, the prospective business owner, and me, a seasoned, experienced business owner and advisor to small businesses. If you're looking for a check list to guide you in starting a business or a source of referrals to reference material, this book is not for you. My goal is to talk to you about what it means to start and run a small business, both positives and negatives. Owning your own business is the most difficult and demanding job you will ever tackle. If you are thinking about starting your own business because you're tired of the hours and demands of your job—or dealing with a bad boss or wanting to do what you want to do not what someone tells you to do; you're probably going to be disappointed in self-employment.

My goal is to give you a clear eye view of self-employment. Also, I will give you tools to evaluate your new business proposition and to evaluate the success of that business. We will go over what you need to look at and think about when starting a new business. Many business failures could have been avoided if the owner had taken the time, before taking the leap to analyze and understand the new business. I will discuss the tools and methods to do that.

The second part of the book will help you manage your business once it is open. We will examine key elements of running a successful small business. This discussion is not industry specific but covers the basics of any business. Many new business owners will have great strengths in one area of the new business but not much knowledge in the other areas of business management. We will talk about that and the risk of new business owners taking on tasks that do not suit them well.

I have both succeeded and failed in my small business ventures. That knowledge of what to do and what to avoid has value to you, the new business owner. Even though my experience was, most likely, not in your industry, all businesses are very similar and have common areas that are keys to success. Following my guidance will not ensure success or prevent failure but should increase the odds of success. The sooner you know some things the better business owner you will make. Always be ready for aid and advice.

Probably the most important elements to success are money (capital not debt) and luck. You can be the most knowledgeable and hardest working entrepreneur who ever started a business and fail. It happens. The more money you have, the more likely that you will succeed. If you're starting on a shoestring, you will need amazing luck to succeed. If those statements sound negative to you, I'm sorry. The reality is that it is easier to fail at a small business venture than to succeed. Does that mean you should not do it? I don't think so. The upside can be life changing. It is about risk and your ability to deal with the often-difficult complications of owning your own business. If you have the stomach for it, it can be the greatest thing you have ever done.

If you know someone who owns their own business, you should talk to them about the downside of being a business owner. They might say it's all great, but I would think most would mention, the bills, the phone calls at night because of a problem, the employee headaches, the disruptions to their business by road construction, weather, government, unruly customers, the mental burden of debt and payroll and on and on. All of that is something to consider.

In most cases employees are a critical key to success. Employees are often the one area business owners resent more than any other. If you cannot deal with employees, their demands, their failures, their complaints; you should not go into a business that is dependent on employees.

You might have been an employee and thought you employer had it made, in some cases that might be true, but in many situations the employer is the one with the weight of the world on their shoulders. You don't see it as an employee because many of the problems running a small business are not visible to the employees.

I've seen many new business entrepreneurs put together an extensive detailed business plan showing every area of the start-up with information about sources and costs, but almost no mention of employees. If a business is employee dependent, and most businesses are to one degree or another, you need to be able to show how you will hire and manage employees. If you don't have a background in managing employees, which would include hiring and firing, this could be a glaring weakness in your start-up.

Of course, your venture might be a one-man band, or maybe all the employees are family members. That can work, but don't expect to borrow money on that kind of plan. A service business where you're the only employee can work, and has worked for many people, but it is not a growth business. I'm not saying don't do that, you should if it fits what you want, but don't expect much support from outside sources.

If you are considering a business venture with employees, extensive equipment investment, or a large inventory, you will need to do a great deal more analysis than a micro business. This is common sense, the more money going into the business the greater the risk (and potential reward) and as such you probably are going to need some financial assistance. The role of money cannot be over emphasized.

My experience as a small business adviser showed me the obvious, the more money you can contribute to your business the greater your chance of success. And I saw the other side, the less money you have the greater the risk of failure.

You want a guarantee of success, have a couple billion dollars in the bank and you will have success. Not because money makes you a better businessperson, it doesn't, but because you can fail and continue to be in business. Many successful businesses failed a couple of times before they finally started making a profit. If you have the money to survive failure, you can reach success.

The opposite is also true. If you don't have any reserve in cash or ability to raise cash, one bad month could end your business. But one of the biggest mistakes new owners make is around credit and debt. If you borrow money to open a business, you have increased the odds of failure. The why is that most debt demands payment on a regular basis, miss one and you now don't control your fate.

The other trap is extending credit to customers. Depending on the type of business you are considering extending some credit may be necessary, but it should be with caution. Even good credit customers can cause problems, not because they won't pay but because your business is drained of cash. This can be especially true if you are growing. Increased revenues are good but if it is on credit the higher your revenues the more you have in outstanding receivables. All your investment capital can quickly be tied up in those receivables. This is one of those decisions that needs to be made before operations begin, will you extend credit or only accept credit cards.

Almost every decision you make will impact cash flow. Understanding all the elements and what it means to not have sufficient cash is important to your success. As I mentioned above, it is often on the second or forth attempt that a business succeeds, much of that has to do with the owner having a better understanding of all the moving parts in the business and being able to set priorities. The best way to speed up that learning curve is to plan. We will be discussing various forms of planning in the next chapters; suffice it to say planning can be the difference between a smooth, successful operation and a financial disaster.

In summary cash is king and planning is queen in the royalty hierarchy of success in a small business. You might have thought your good idea was all you needed, trust me; it is not. Plenty of capital and good luck will drive success much more than the "best idea in the world." The only way to offset the lack of huge piles of cash is planning. The more you plan the more you understand. Time spent planning and preparing pays off in good results and money in the bank.

2

Evaluating Your Idea.

A lot of good business ideas just come out of the blue. You're thinking about something else and bam there is that "great idea" for a business. Now do those turn out to be the most successful, no way of knowing. A lot of good business ideas are not much more than a slight improvement to an existing business. So, you look at a business in your town experiencing success and say, "I can make that better!" Business ideas do not have to be original or unique; if you can show an improvement on an existing business that might be the best way to go.

Of course, brand new businesses can happen. You might be a computer guy who has an idea that nobody has ever done. First piece of advice --don't tell people about your idea, unless you really, really trust them or they have signed a non-disclosure agreement. New innovative business concepts have appeal but also can cause issues. One, of course, is that it is new. Sounds stupid but new ideas have no comparisons. You can say, hey my new idea is just like X; but if it isn't how can anyone judge the viability of this new idea. Unless you have a history of building companies based on innovation, you might find most people skeptical of your "new idea".

Whatever your business concept you need to evaluate its likelihood of success. This evaluation might be as simple as talking to people with knowledge in the industry, or seeking advice from other experts, or just spending time yourself trying to test the chances of success on paper before jumping in. There is no one path in this process or a one and only way to go. It may depend on your idea, or it may depend on your resources, such as money to pay fees to others.

Whenever I have a business idea, my first step is to "run the numbers." If you have this ability, the best approach is to build a spreadsheet so that you can test various assumptions. Let's use as a model an idea for a restaurant called Bob's Deli. Bob has been in the restaurant business for some years and has decided to try self-employment. His background in the fundamentals of the business is good but he lacks management experience. He thinks his kitchen skills far outweigh his lack of running the business experience. How should he evaluate his chances of success?

Bob decides he knows enough that he can put together a spreadsheet that will help him understand the details of this new business. He begins with assumptions about customer counts. He labels his columns as Day, Week, Month and Year. What drives every aspect of his new business is customers. So, to even start to analyze his idea he must make an educated guess on the number of customers his new business can attract. At this point he also will have to assume how he is going to market his business. He might have one assumption if he was planning on spending a million dollars in preopening marketing, as opposed to a couple of hundred targeting social media. Bob doesn't have a million dollars, so his customer count numbers are mostly based on word of mouth.

His experience tells him that most restaurants will attract customers who are curious about the new business and want to try it. Base on that experience and his almost non-existent marketing budget he makes his assumptions about customer counts per day, working that into week, month, and year.

With that he can start to build the spreadsheet. He makes

educated guesses on what the average customer will buy, that works into projecting revenue. Using his knowledge of what good food cost should be for his type of restaurant he can build his projected direct costs. This will give him a gross profit number after deducting his direct food costs. From there he looks at other costs, such as labor, overhead (which includes rent, insurance, utilities, advertising and any and all expenses he can think of). Once all these assumptions are made, he can calculate profit or loss on a daily basis and roll that into the other periods.

Bob has been honest in his estimates. He didn't try to fudge anything one way or another. He used his experience, and a little research to put together his best guesses. At this point his numbers are going to show a profit or a loss. Now he analyzes his assumptions. He looks at all the elements; are they reasonable, not to optimistic or pessimistic. Once he determines he thinks they are good projections, what does he know?

If it's a loss, he must stop and try to figure out why. Are the revenues numbers reasonable? If the only way you can get your spreadsheet to reflect a profit is to assume unrealistic revenue; you might want to reconsider your business venture.

How about if this shows fantastic profits? Don't believe them. Test each assumption and see if there are flaws.

The process of building spreadsheet may take hours to days to months. But once you have a working model of you new venture you can start testing every assumption to show where the business must reach to be successful. A key number to know would be the break-even point. What are the assumptions at break-even, how many customers and how much does each spend to reach that number?

A critical point to mention is paying yourself. You can skew the numbers by either assuming you are working at lower-than-normal wages or higher than normal wages. You should establish a market value cost of a manager, not what you want to make, but what it would take to hire someone else to do the job.

If you have included market rates for all workers (not family members rates) and the model is showing a profit, the next step is to measure that projected profit against the investment you are contributing. As an example, if you invested $100,000 you would want a minimum return on that investment. Might be 6% or 10%, you would decide what is the minimum you think is reasonable. So, if that was 6% you would want your model to show a profit of $6,000 after paying a reasonable salary to you for running the business.

The more you work with this business model, the better you will understand your future business. I know many people are not "numbers" people and this becomes tedious if not impossible work. My advice is that if you feel you cannot build this financial model, you should hire someone to do it. This does not have to be some high dollar accountant; it can be your cousin or niece. They know how to use spreadsheets, but they cannot make the assumptions about the numbers to build the sheet. You must do that based on your research or experience.

Now there are people who advise start-ups that can help, but it costs. My advice to all new business owners is to try to do most of the analysis of your business yourself, with help as needed. Not only do you become more familiar with the inner workings of a business, but you learn much about how to manage a business.

Back to Bob's Deli. Bob can at once see that a two-percentage point increase in food costs almost wipes out all his profit. Working the numbers makes that obvious. He will now know going into running the business that he has to watch food costs and if they are too high take some action. He can either increase prices, which of course, could lower sales, or cut costs. Often in the restaurant business this is about controlling wastes. If your employees are not paying attention, your food costs can increase just through sloppiness. It's not just good business practice to pay attention to the numbers, it is fundamental to having a successful business.

It's not just the restaurant business, every business can be modeled. Using financial modeling spreadsheets gives you a head start on understanding the factors driving financial success. Of course, it is all based on assumptions, and everyone knows what that means. But even making those assumptions about customers, revenues, and costs start the process of understanding your business before it is actual dollars out the backdoor. Planning is a way to see your business running without any risk of actual loss.

Evaluating and understanding your business before actual operations is a valuable tool. The effort involved is, I think, a real key to success.

3

Numbers to Know.

Okay, we are saying planning and evaluation are critical to success. What are the numbers you need to know to make the most of those efforts? This is going to sound simple, but it is not. You need to know what revenues to expect.

In the example of Bob's Deli, we had a pretty good idea on what to expect in revenues based on his experience in a similar business. Now that does not mean Bob assumed the correct number, more than likely he did not, but it means he was in the ballpark.

If the business was a new service company, providing a unique service no one has ever heard of; how in the world would you be able to predict revenues. The quick and honest answer is you can't. Now what?

A good approach, if you are stuck in making assumptions about revenues, is to build a spreadsheet on expenses and costs. Using Bob's as an example. First you would put together your known costs—usually this is overhead or fixed costs. Name everything you can think of; utilities, insurance, rent, etc. At that point the next step would depend on your type of business. A retail store, or a food service, or a service business will all have their own characteristics that will have to be developed.

For Bob's it would be food costs or gross margin after food costs. Labor costs would be both fixed, such as a manager, and variable, for most of the staff. With those numbers you can back into what revenues must be to reach break-even.

A service business would of course not have food costs and

would be driven more by labor costs. A retail business would have gross margin percentage which would be the cost of products sold. Manufacturing would be a whole different animal with lots of complications. While much of this may sound like gobbledygook it is important as a business owner to understand how all these numbers affect your ability to make a profit and therefore a living.

Okay, at this point you are thinking, I don't want to be an accountant. Fair enough. But if you want to be successful, you will need to know these numbers. Many decisions will be based on understanding your key numbers and how they affect the business. You can hire someone to do this for you, but like many things, you only really understand something if you do it yourself.

Messing around with numbers is not something most people enjoy but give it a try. For Bob's restaurant he first tried to estimate the number of customers per day. Bob had experience in a similar business which was about the same size as what his was going to be, so he had some good ideas. If he hadn't, he might have tried going around to some businesses that were similar and asking. Now this can be tricky. Walking into a business and asking how many customers they average per day probably will get you thrown out. My advice is to be honest. "I'm thinking about opening my own restaurant and was wondering if you could give me a little advice?" Your chances of finding a business owner or employee willing to give you some information is probably about 50 percent. I have found in my experience that many business owners are eager to talk about their business and offer advice. You will need to make it clear you are not planning on opening next door, but if you can say you are considering a location across town on in another city, they might open-up and tell you all their secrets.

It is helpful in that investigative step if you understand the numbers beforehand. The better you understand the key numbers the more meaningful your conversations with people in the industry. Let's stick with the restaurant industry and look at their key numbers.

- Number of customers per day. This is an average and will be used to develop revenue projections. This is one of those numbers that most other businesses owners should be willing to share, there are no proprietary secrets involved here. A services business and retail would also be driven by number of customers. Manufacturing might have a key number that is units shipped per day. Of course, it is understood that the number varies each day, we are just looking for an average.
- Average revenue per customer. In case of Bobs, he might break it down to average food sales per customer, average drink sales or other categories. In other industries, such as retail, your customer per day might be broken down into categories, such as average toy customer per day, average game customer per day and so on. Whatever category you have average customer broken out you would now need average sale per category.
- Direct Cost per each category. For Bobs this is direct food costs. Whatever perishable food items go into making his product. This will include oils, condiments, and everything that is directly involved in making Bobs products.
- Indirect Costs. This is still food costs but not direct costs. This would be paper goods, such as napkins, containers, cups. Anything that is variable with number of sales tied directly to the food product.
- Labor Costs. Cost of labor is a huge cost in most businesses. Some labor is fixed, such as a manager's salary, but most labor is variable. The higher the revenue projections the more labor needed to accommodate those customers. One of the easiest

ways to build into this number is to develop a staffing schedule. Once you have hours needed to meet the revenue numbers you can add wages and come up with costs. Included in labor costs should be employer labor taxes and unemployment insurance.
- Other Variable Costs/Expenses. This will generally be very specific to the business not the industry. Something like a rent that involves paying a percent of sales would be included here. A manager's bonus based on revenue might be included in this category. Each business will be different.
- Fixed Overhead. These items tend to be consistent each month. There could some variability, such as utilities, but usually if it is not tied to revenue they are included in fixed expenses. The big items are rent, insurance, advertising/marketing, utilities, communication services (phone, internet), safety, security, and cleaning supplies.

Every industry will have their own set of items in that list. Each business will have a unique set of items. But almost all businesses will have many common items. As a new business owner, you need to know those numbers.

You don't need to know them as an accountant would, but you need to know how they affect your business. Do they vary with sales? How does payroll change my insurance costs? Are my assumptions about food costs too high or too low? What are industry standards for all these categories? As a percentage of sales?

A lot to know and think about. If you want to be successful, this is one of the keys, understanding these numbers. Can you be successful without knowing any of this? Yes. No question there are business owners who do not understand the relationship of these numbers to their business. They may rely upon an accountant, or spouse, or buddy to know this stuff and tell them what they need to know. Will that work? Yes. Is it best? No.

In many small businesses the difference between success and failure is often small things. Food cost being 3 percentage points too high, fixed overhead not matching with revenues by a few hundred dollars per month. Labor costs being too high. It may surprise you but seldom is failure based on poor sales. Oh, sure that happens. Terrible location or poor parking and the business is doing half what was expected. But in my experience, most businesses are achieving their revenue goals but not making money because the owner is not managing all the details in the everyday operations that need to be controlled. Success comes from paying attention to the details. To do that you have to understand those details and know when they are wrong and how to fix it.

You can rely on other people, accountant, or bookkeeper, to provide you with the detail you need, but to really understand what all that means you need to be hands-on and develop a working understanding of what these numbers mean. I don't want you to become an accountant, which would be counterproductive, but you need to think like one on many occasions.

4
How Much Money?

You have now spent time analyzing and thinking about all the elements of your new business. You have developed a financial model that tells you it is a good idea to proceed. So, how much money are you going to need to open this business? Quick and easy answer, a hell of a lot!

Remember, money is the biggest key to success. The more money you have the greater your chance to succeed. Why? Because you would have the resources to fail and try again. If you have the minimum to start and you hit a bump in the road, you most likely will be out of business before you can make the changes and correct the mistakes you made at the beginning.

I have often referred to this as having access to dad money. Now if that offends anyone, I'm sorry. But it's the truth. If you have a rich dad, willing to back-up your business venture, your chances for success go up dramatically. Without dad money, when the shit hits the fan, well nothing happens, no rescue, just business failure.

Now, if you don't have access to "dad money", you will need a lot more than you thought. If you based your money assumptions on the cost of equipment and maybe a couple of months of overhead. The slightest blip will put you under.

Enough doom and gloom, can you open a business on a shoestring and succeed? Yes. Many businesses have done exactly that. There are tons of stories about borrowing $500 from your roommate and starting a business that today is worth millions. Many of those stories are lies, but some are true. Remember the other key factor in business success, luck. If you're lucky enough miracles can happen.

Another issue with money is that you can borrow whatever you need. Not so! Unless, of course, the lender is Dad. In the real world you can only borrow the money if you have a proven source of payback and adequate collateral. There are many of business ventures that have been financed based on equity in a house and the spouse's income. If you have that set of circumstances, then being able to borrow may exist. Keep in mind many homes have been lost due to business failures financed with home equity.

In most cases a new business will be financed with equity capital and debt. Equity capital will come from the business owner, or his family, or his friends and on rare occasions investors. It is not common to have investors who are not family or friends. The reason it is rare is that most small business start-ups fail, so for investors the risk is too high. If the risk is so high, should I be opening my own business? Good question, you might want to think about that.

We will go deeper into where to find the money in the next chapter. Let's stick to how much money.

What is needed to open the doors to your new business. Time for a list? Bob's restaurant will need equipment, freezers, refrigerator, grill, fryers, and much more. He will need furniture, tables, and chairs. He will need signage, menu board, outdoor sign for the front, miscellaneous signs. He will need other equipment, computers, phones, safe etc. So, Bob's list might look like this:

1. Kitchen Equipment $20,000
2. Front Equipment $5,000
3. Dining Equipment/furniture $10,000

4. Signage $7,000
5. Leasehold Improvements $12,000
6. Other Miscellaneous $5,000

Bob's list totals $59,000. He also estimated that he would need about $6,000 in inventory, including some retail items he was planning to have in his store. So, is $65,000 what Bob needs to open his business? Probably not.

Bob thinks he will need 60 days to complete his improvements in his new restaurant. So, there will be a couple of months' rent before he opens. Also, there will be several deposits requirement. That looks like another $6,000. Also, he plans to have some employees on board before the store opens for training and getting everything ready. Added payroll before day 1 is estimated at $4,000. Bob of course, needs to pay himself before any revenue is coming in, he thinks he can get by with an added $5,000.

Bob's number is now $80,000. Bob is in an industry that usually opens with strong sales so he thinks after he is open, he will start to make a profit, but to be safe he thinks he should have an added $10,000 in working capital as a cushion. Bob is very wise.

So, Bob's total cost to open is $90,000. He thinks he can get his supplier of equipment to finance 50% of the equipment and furniture cost or $15,000 in debt. Now he needs $75,000 in cash. Bob has $25,000 in savings leaving him short $50,000. We will look at options to raise that money in the next chapter.

Is Bob's estimate of $90,000 to start his business, correct? Probably. He did a good job in calculating some of the normally overlooked items, such as rent before you open the doors, labor before revenue begins and a general cushion (reserve for contingencies). If Bob's restaurant is profitable from day one, he is probably in good shape financially. Congratulations Bob.

This is the area that cannot be known. What happens once the doors are open. Bob has done the work and based all his assumptions on projected customer count and the revenue that generates. What if Bob was wrong? This is the biggest risk of a new business, you completely overestimated revenues. At that point everything becomes a challenge. You must adjust on the fly to offset costs/expenses to try to match to the new revenue numbers. Difficult at best, and in many cases impossible.

In a seminar setting covering some of this same material, I had someone say, “this just shows there is no reason to do any of that planning, you just wait and see what it is and try to figure out how to survive.” In some ways he might be right, but he missed the point. If you had done the analysis and came up with these real bad revenue numbers in your projection, you would not have opened the business in the first place. The analysis is not to prove what you want it to be, but what you think based on your best analysis it is going to be.

Take this scenario of opening and feeling the failure on day one to heart. How would you feel? This is important to remember when you’re doing your planning, you are planning so you can avoid this pit in your stomach feeling. Sure, most business owners dream of opening and having huge success day one. Within a year they have opened two more locations and life is wonderful, but business is full of risk, and you should also consider the downside.

Is there any way to calculate what amount of money you should have to allow for an adjustment period of loss? Probably not. But if you did, it would no doubt almost double the amount you first came up with and, for most people, that would make the amount required to open impossible.

Bob tried to mitigate the risk by including some numbers for costs before opening. That gave him a range of capital needed before any debt of $65,000 to $90,000. The amount borrowed can of course reduce this cash requirement, but debt is its own problem. Even if you can borrow more, based on collateral other than your home, debt must be paid back, which usually involves regular payments every month.

Often new business owners will start to cut corners at this point and decide they can make it on a lower amount. Say for Bob, he might decide he can get the store opened faster, cut out some of the equipment, lease some of the equipment at a premium but reducing cash and come up with a new number of $40,000. Leaving him $15,000 short, which he thinks he can get from friends and family by promising them a guaranteed return on their money. He is digging a deeper hole, which might be impossible to get out of.

A business owner should never underestimate what it takes to open their new business. They are only hurting themselves, if anything, it would be safer to overestimate. But human nature is what it is, and often we fool ourselves into believing what we want to believe.

This book is about how to open a successful business, it is not about how to open an unsuccessful business. The keys are money and luck. But what a business owner can control to help both of those is good planning and honest planning. If you do the hard work of planning, you should see that you increase your risk dramatically trying to open a business on a shoestring. As we have said before it has happened. People have started businesses with little money and reached huge success, but for sure they had an extra helping of luck to be able to overcome the lack of capital. Planning on being super lucky is no plan at all.

5
Where is the Money?

Willie Sutton, an infamous bank robber in the 1930s, was asked, why do you rob banks, he replied, "because that's where the money is."

That may be our answer also. If you are looking to borrow money for your business venture, your first stop should be banks. It's what they supposedly do, loan money. Now many banks only loan money to people who don't need it, so they may not be interested in your project. Some banks will only loan money to small business start-ups through the SBA due to the risk associated with every start-up. There is nothing wrong with the SBA option.

All lenders, whether loan shark or the biggest bank in town, look at the same things. Collateral and ability to pay back whatever you're borrowing. A start-up business has no history for anything, much less a sufficient cash flow to repay a loan. Banks love real estate as collateral, for the obvious reasons and some not so obvious. I once had a banker tell me that they always took some position on a borrower's house if it was a new business so that the borrow was motivated to pay them back first. I have an opinion on bankers, but we won't discuss it here.

The SBA programs work but you will still have to meet standard requirements for a loan, this is not a grant program. The advantage with the SBA is the banks are willing to take more risk and offer longer-term loans. If you are looking to borrow money this is an avenue you should explore. The best approach to learn what you need is the SBA web site and then visiting a local banker. There are also some good lenders on the internet doing

SBA loans. Google will give you those web sites.

The planning and worksheets we have discussed would be the basis for any loan and specifically an SBA application. The more detailed your analysis, the better the bank will understand your business proposal which will improve your chances of securing a loan. Note, that none of these loans are made without your personal guarantee. You may have incorporated your business, but the banks and the SBA will require you and in most cases your spouse to guarantee all loans.

Every banker will be happy to share with you the horror stories of failure that is common with new small business start-ups, and it is true. Don't be offended if they suggest your chances are slim, it is what it is. These are generally people who have avoided risk in their lives and don't understand why you are taking on this risk, but that does not matter, you know why you are doing it, that is what matters.

Beyond banks there are many personal loan lenders. These are often referred to as signature loans. They are based almost exclusively on your credit score, although there can be income requirements. If the lender requires income, your new business potential income will not be considered. If your spouse has employment income that might suffice with good credit for a decent size loan, this is worth considering; however, the downside is that the rates are going to be higher and the term shorter than a bank. It's not the borrowing money that is the problem, it's the paying back.

There are shadier lenders that do exist. Stay away. There is no reason to finance a new business under threat of personal harm. Find a good job and save.

The new business owner's fantasy is finding investors. This very seldom happens. There are all sorts of things happening on the internet. Some sources through that channel may exist, but

I would approach with caution. Real, independent investors will almost never invest in a new small business start-up. We know the reason, it is risk. Small business failure rate is high and there are many ways to invest money that can be safer and generate better returns than a small business venture.

Most "real" investors in small business are in two groups, family, and friends. Ah, we're back to Dad money!

Why would family and friends be willing to invest in your business? You. Yep, no pressure at all, the only reason most would invest is because they want to help you. You can pretend they are making a wise investment decision but that is not true. They may believe in your abilities and think they will make their money back, but most will write it off once they hand over the money.

Now if you can actually create a return for your family and friend investors, you will find more family and friends who will want in on the next opportunity.

Some money might be raised with equipment financing, usually through the seller of the equipment. This can be loans or leasing. If your business is equipment intensive this might be a way to access needed equipment while avoiding banks or family and friends. But it is only for equipment and nothing for other needs.

For small business start-ups the best and most logical source of money is you. Savings, retirement funds, home equity, personal loans, these are the most likely sources of capital to start a business. Some of these sources come with significant downside risk. Using your house or your retirement money to finance a business puts a great deal more pressure on you to succeed. Failure means some very bad outcomes. I know this for a fact, I've been there.

Anyone who is considering going into business for themselves is more than likely not in a position where they can honestly analyze the risk. Bob's restaurant venture, according to Bob was the greatest idea since McDonald's. A sure thing. No risk at all. Everyone else, except Bob, knew there was great risk. Even if Bob was the best restaurant person in the world, the risk was very high, because small businesses fail at a very high rate.

If business failure means you lose your house, your retirement money, all your cash, or your family and friend investors hate you, failure becomes a tragedy. It's not a bad business deal, it's the complete destruction of your life. Give that some serious thought before you jump in with both feet.

Another avenue that is high risk would be the allure of credit cards. If you have good credit, there is the opportunity to build a large portfolio of credit cards. Many small businesses will fall victim to this trap and run up credit cards trying to meet the surprises that pop up. This is incredibly expensive debt and with only a few exceptions, will cause more grief than benefit.

If you save the money to start your business, you will be motivated to succeed and you will not have debt pressure. Of course, saving enough to start a business is difficult for most of us. While difficult this is the path I would recommend. Some amount of your savings should be a part of the money needed to start, the more the better. Even if you're going to depend on family money you should contribute what you can to your venture. Investment can be a strong motivator to work hard for success.

In order of preference, I would go with personal funds as number one. I know this is hard but saving money might be the safest path to success. Next would-be family, notice I left out friends. Family money can create problems if the business is not a success or can create problems if the business is a big success. But families handle these problems differently than outsiders. It is you second best option. Third would be banks with SBA backing. I think every new business should explore this option for capital. The rates are lower than other options and the terms are longer. Another advantage of just applying for these loans is the requirement for a detail analysis of the new venture. It forces you to plan and think about your new business and to be able to present it to someone else, who is going to be skeptical and ask hard questions.

Finding money to start a small business is probably the most difficult part of the whole experience. Money is the major factor in success. The more you have, under the right structure, the more likely you will succeed. Starting a business on a shoestring is a proven formula for failure. And, I'm sorry, but there are no easy answers when it comes to money, unless you just have a boat load laying around somewhere. And if that is true, you probably don't want to start a small business. Do your homework and understand your new business in detail and then start the process of getting the money you need, it's not easy.

6
Structure.

What is the best legal structure for a new small business? It depends. Yep, no straightforward answers on any of this stuff.

The simplest structure is as a sole proprietorship. There is no legal paperwork associated with this form of business. You just start. Many small businesses, especially service businesses, are sole proprietorships. It works. Tax filing is easy. No government involvement in setting up your business. So, it's easy, what's wrong with this approach. Usually, the downside is protecting the name of your business and limiting personal liability. You can protect the name by filing with (usually) the Secretary of State in your state for a trade name. Depending on your business your personal liability might be very small, or you can mitigate that risk with liability insurance. Easiest for sure, with few if any forms to fill out, however, I do not recommend this approach.

To make a more serious statement requires the formation of an entity for your new business. I think the two best choices are a Limited Liability Company and a Corporation. We'll go over both of those. Keep in the mind the more people involved, such as investors, the need to have some legal advice increases. You may think Uncle Frank would be the last guy who would sue you but think again. Even with family members if you are taking other people's money you should get legal advice on how to handle that and the best legal structure for all involved.

If the business will be yourself and maybe a spouse, the best legal structure might be an LLC. For one these are super simple to form. No need for an elaborate legal document. In most states you can supply the needed information in a matter of minutes on-line. You name must be unique, but this process will also protect your name for use in the state you filed the LLC. For tax purposes this is a pass-through entity, meaning that the business entity does not pay taxes they are paid by the members of the entity. If that is just yourself, then you pay taxes on the earnings of the company as your income. No separate tax return, you would just file a schedule C to record the revenue, expenses, and taxable income.

Another significant advantage of an LLC is that there is no requirement for support documents to keep the legality of the entity. Such as the requirement for board of directors' minutes in a corporation. The LLC will provide a similar limit on personal liability as a corporation but all that goes out the window in case of fraud. Once again let me emphasize that depending on your circumstances you should seek legal advice. If you are wealthy and own a lot of assets you would want to have a conversation with an attorney on how to best protect your personal assets from the actions of the new company. And, of course, if you are wealthy then you can afford to pay for that advice. For people who don't have as much, and maybe everything you have is tied up in this new business venture, the need to protect non-existing assets is not too high.

A corporation is another legal entity that can be a good route to set up your new business. The forms are more complicated but not a huge burden. In the past attorneys used to make a nice little fee off forming corporations but today you can do it all on-line with standardize forms and meet all legal requirements without paying much at all. Of course, in the past those attorneys would give you a fancy minute book and an official seal. Most of that stuff has gone away, but a lot of the requirements for making sure your separate legal structure is providing you with a liability barrier from your personal assets requires many documents be kept on a regular basis. You should have regular meetings with the required board members present. These meetings should be recorded, and minutes kept. If that is just you and maybe a spouse that starts to get silly. What happens is you stop with the silliness and do not keep good records. Then if something happens and you want to say you are not personally liable only the corporation, but you don't have the docs to back-up that this was a "real" corporation, those same attorneys can penetrate the liability shield and go after your personal assets.

Many small businesspeople will form a corporation because they like having Inc. after the business name. Or it gives them a sense of status within the family. Shut up big brother, I'm now the CEO of Little Company, Inc.

The form you take for your business will depend on a lot of different factors. The most important is to protect your personal assets if you have any. Or to protect yourself from legal requirements if you have outside investors. Also, the self-image aspect is real. You may want to deal with the added paperwork burden of a corporation if it gives you an ego boost to be the head of a tiny corporation.

The corporation can also be a pass-through entity for taxes by filing to be a sub-chapter S corporation. The Corporation will still have to file a separate tax return, but the owner or owners will be taxed for the corporation earnings on their individual tax returns—even if the funds were not distributed.

As I said before my general advice is to first look to an LLC if you are not going to have outside investors. You can still do the LLC with outside investors, but it can become a bit more awkward. The more investors you have, the more likely you would look at a corporation. Also, investors mean you should seek legal advice about all of this.

The structure of your company has almost nothing to do with achieving success in your new business venture, but it is important to think about these matters at the beginning. Each new business owner will have their own set of circumstances that will impact the decision on what structure is best for your new business. If this is an area that completely baffles you seek advice. One thing you will learn, if you're paying attention, is that you will not know everything about being in business. You will eventually develop a team of advisors for the matters that you do not have the knowledge to deal with yourself. Legal issues require lawyers, accounting and tax issues requires accountants and CPAs, advertising, marketing issues may require people with specialized talents—there are few businesses that can be one-man bands; develop a team approach to the areas where you are less skilled, and you will increase your chances of success.

7
Escape Hatch?

Many new business owners will soon discover that they have created a bad job for themselves. You pour your life savings into your new business venture and now you are working 10- and 12-hour days 6 days a week and sometimes 7. How much money would you have demanded from a boss for such dedication and sacrifice? Maybe there was no amount of money that would entice you into this slave like existence. It was your dream to own your own business, but now it is your worst nightmare.

This can happen. This does happen. Now what? This is not what you want to do, but before you make up your mind about going into your own business, think about this worst-case scenario. Let's call this your escape hatch plan.

How do you get out? Back to Bob's restaurant. Bob is sick and tired of the hours. He's making something less than minimum wage. They only way he can survive is take a job with someone else. He has failed but he doesn't want to starve. What are his options?

First, let's be candid. You may want to just skip this chapter because you are not going to fail. Well, of course, no one plans on failing—except, maybe, some sports teams, but it happens. Because it happens, even to nice, hardworking people like Bob, you should read this chapter. Why, because if you fail it would be best if you have thought about how to minimize your losses. That is what we are doing, helping you visualize some options now; not waiting until disaster strikes.

Option One—Bob goes to work for someone else. Let's assume that Bob can go get a high-paying job working for someone else. He doesn't want to do that, but money is money, and he needs a lot. Bob thinks he can just let the existing staff run the business and he can be available on weekends, or they can call in emergencies. Without his cost to the business, he thinks the operation will make a slight profit even with the poor revenue numbers that created this whole mess.

Bob has solved one problem, his need for more money, by taking a job, but he has created other problems. His employees have never been in charge of every decision about the business, plus they resent the fact that Bob, the owner, is not there when there are problems. They feel abandoned and want more money. If Bob pays his existing employees more money, he is lessening the benefit of not paying himself. He tells his employees that he cannot pay them more and if they don't like it, they can quit, which some immediately do. Bob must hire more employees and takes a few days off to interview. His new boss tells Bob that if he can't show up every day, he will have to fire him. Bob hires the first people that show up even though he's not sure they know what they are doing. Soon, the business is doing half of what it was when Bob was there, the number of bad reviews skyrockets and includes some ugly stuff. This choice did not work.

Option Two—Bob tries to sell the business; first to his brother-in-law (Jim) and second through a business broker. Jim tells Bob the business is so bad now the only way he would consider anything is if Bob put in $30,000 cash so Jim would have time to fix the mess. The conversation ends in a yelling match. Bob's sister calls and curses Bob for being so rude to her husband. The business broker laughs at Bob and suggests he might find someone to take over the lease if Bob leaves all the equipment. Bob said things to the business broker he wanted to say to Jim, but Jim was family.

Option Three—Bob files for bankruptcy. Bob had put up his house so his family will have to move. Bob could keep his car since he needed it to get to his new job. Bob cursed the day he opened Bob's restaurant. Bob becomes a good employee and never complains. Soon Bob's wife leaves him saying he was a poor provider.

There is no escape hatch for a failing business. If your business is doing well, you could possibly sell it, but if it is doing well you would want to keep it. Catch-22. The only way out of the mess is for Bob to have a huge pile of money somewhere. Bob doesn't and most business owners don't. Everything gets tied up in the business venture.

Would you invest $10,000 dollars and be happy making 10 bucks? Of course not. This is the most critical analysis you will make about your new business adventure. Do the rewards justify the risks?

The risks are huge, as we can see with Bob, it usually means total collapse. But often it is total collapse financially and emotionally. Families break up over business failures. Divorces and lawsuits are some of the outcomes when a business fails.

There is no way to put numbers to this. We have already discussed analyzing the business to make sure you want to do this, so you did it, because the numbers said it would make a profit, life would be good. But you were wrong. You miscalculated, or something changed. The new competitor that opened next door who took all your customers. The government decided to close the road to your business for six months to fix the sewer. Disaster on top of disaster and you failed. If you could have seen that, you would not have gone into the business. Everything you did in your analysis said it was a good decision to start this business, but it wasn't.

Rather than numbers, you should write down what would happen if you failed. If your house is part of the collateral that is the first thing to write down—lose house. Continue that list until you have thought of ever consequence you can associate with failing in this new business venture. And then think about what all of that really means. Think about the pain and the ugly words, if you have investors, think about the lawsuits and the screaming matches. Think about how this will affect your personal life, marriage, kids and on and on.

Keep that list. This is the ugly side of self-employment, what does failure really mean. The title of this chapter is Escape Hatch with a question mark. Is there an escape hatch? For most people the answer is no. Oh, you'll get out and you will live. But the costs can be incredibly high, not just in money but in many personal ways.

One of the first things we talked about was the importance of money. If you have a ton of money you will succeed. Without it, your chances of failure go up, way up. Now for many of us if we had the money, we wouldn't go into business for ourselves, if we had enough, we would invest in something secure and just live, but that doesn't work for all of us.

What drives most entrepreneurs is not money (you may not believe that, but I do), it is accomplishment. Success is measured in money; it is also measured in that wonderful feeling you have when you succeed.

Look at and think about all of this. Is the risk work it? Can you take the heat if you fail? Are you risking more than you willing to lose?

Give it a lot of thought before you say, "Let's GO!"

8

Business Plan—Yes, or No?

In past years, the next thing you would tackle would be a business plan. This is the tool that will ultimately decide if you are going to open this business, the tool you will use to secure debt, the tool you will use to impress investors, the document you will use in lease negotiations and many other ways.

Today, many people say you don't need a formalized business plan. It takes too much time, it is most likely not very accurate, who cares anyway, just show us the numbers? Some of that is true, it does take a lot of time. I personally think it is another good investment of time and money leading up to the decision to start a business. As you can see a bunch of my advice on opening a business is to analyze the decision in many ways. The more you look and think about the business the better prepared you will be to be in business.

A business plan can be especially hard because in most cases it is written. I've met people who could talk about their business idea for hours but ask them to write a short synopsis and it stops them dead in their tracks. This can be that they are not comfortable with writing, but I think it is more than that. We can talk and speak in generalities and vagueness, and it sounds like detail, but when you write it down, it requires more preciseness. It's hard to write a business plan and maybe that's the reason you should write one.

Have you ever listened to someone give a speech and think it was okay but look at the transcript and realized they didn't really say anything? Written words are not as forgiving as spoken words. My advice is do a business plan; I think it will pay off.

How To Write A Business Plan. The business plan should tell a reader what your business is about—what it does, who are the people behind the business, how it all works and why the business exists. The plan is a tool --like a map. For it to be the most useful, it should set specific goals and aims.

Prepare an outline. The plan should tell your story—it should be kept precise and focused. Number of pages is not important; readability and concise presentation of information is the most important aspect.

Basic Outline

- Cover
- Table of Contents
- Executive Summary
- Business Description
- Definition of the Market/Industry
- Description of Products/Services
- Organization and Management
- Marketing and Sales
- Financial

Executive Summary. Short concise summary of your plan. This should be written last—this is not the plan—it should not be more than two pages. However, there are some readers of your plan who will only read the Executive Summary—therefore, it is very important that you highlight the key elements of your plan. The primary goal of the executive summary is to have your reader want to learn more.

Business Description. This section can have a mission statement (business purpose) and a vision of the company in the future. Mission statements should not be statements of personal philosophy but a statement that relates to what the business is supposed to accomplish. This section would have the business goals and objectives, a brief history of the business and a list of key company employees. A clear statement of the company's potential is a vital part of this section.

Definition of the Market. Here you would describe your business industry and its outlook. Define the critical needs of your perceived or existing market. Find your target market. Supply a general profile of your targeted clients/customers. What share of the market do you currently have or expect to have. The reader will want to know how your business is fulfilling the needs of customers within this market.

Description of Products or Services. Describe your product and/or services. This should have sufficient detail for your reader to know what you are going to be supplying or selling. Explain the competitive advantages in the marketplace. Describe how the product or service meets the needs of the targeted customers. Include price information and how it fits within the competitive market. Include photos, sales material or drawings.

Organization and Management. How is the business organized? Supply an organizational chart. Describe the legal structure of your business (sole proprietor, partnership, LLC, Corporation etc.) Describe any special license, registrations or permits that would be needed. Provide brief biographical information on each key member of the management team

Marketing and Sales Strategy. This section should:

- Identify and describe your market—who your customers are and what the demand is for your products and services.
- Describe your channels of distribution.
- Explain your sales strategy, specific to pricing, promotion, products and place (4Ps).

After reviewing this section, the reader should know:

- Who your market is and how you will reach it.
- How your company will apply pricing, promotion, product diversification and channel distribution to sell your products and services competitively.

Financial Management

This section should include:

For a New Business

- Estimate of start-up costs.
- Projected balance sheet (1 year forward).
- Projected income statement (1 year forward).
- Projected cash flow statement (12 months forward).

For an Existing Business

- Balance sheets (last 3 years).
- Income statements (last 3 years).
- Cash flow statement (12 months).

If Applying for a Loan (in addition to the above)

- Current personal financial statement on each principal.
- Federal tax return for prior year.

After reviewing the Financial Management section, the reader should:

- Have a good understanding about the financial ability and/or projections for your company.

An important aspect to remember about a business plan is that it is your document. Don't just write it to support a loan request, or for potential investors, write it for yourself. Once it is done, keep it up to date. On a regular basis review the plan and make changes to improve the plan to match what has happen with your business. This is a working document not some throwaway.

I know this can be difficult. In some ways that is the point. Completing this difficult task helps you develop a true plan. Putting your thoughts and ideas on paper helps you organize them into a logical plan that can be understood by the reader. Emphasize your knowledge and enthusiasm for this venture. This does not have to be a boring document of facts and figures, let your passion come through to your reader.

9

Look, Analyze, Think, Re-think before Taking the Plunge.

This is probably starting to sound like a broken record, never stop planning and analyzing. This is the last step before you start the hard work of getting your business up and running. Take a few hours, or a few days and re-think everything.

You're close to your goal of opening your own business, have you done everything that you could to improve your odds of success. If you have a trusted friend, associate, family member ask them to give you their honest opinion on what you are about to do. This, of course, can be dangerous. Honesty is something we want in theory, but we really want approval. Listen and try and take in all the information you can and then review again to see if you are ready to be self-employed.

I have often recommended that new entrepreneurs stop at this point and question yourself. If you have not signed a lease or made commitments to employees, you might want to consider backing out. If something inside you is saying, "I'm not ready," then stop and wait. All the time you have spent getting ready is not wasted. If you decide to wait, your next step should be to get a job in whatever industry you're thinking about jumping into. You would find that your whole perspective about work will have changed. You will pay attention to the small details, because this is the ultimate research. Work in your industry as an employee, but an employee who is paying attention to what it would feel like if you owned the business. Do that for a year or maybe even five years, until you can say with confidence, "I'm ready!"

Another approach I highly recommend, if you are questioning the timing, is to look for a partner. Maybe you're great with employees and customers but not good at details. Could be finding a partner who is good at details will create a dream team destined for success. Or maybe the money worries you, maybe someone with a bit of cash as a working partner might make sense. Don't be stubborn, keep your eyes open to possibilities that will improve your odds of success.

If at this point you are sure you have done everything you should have to evaluate and understand your new business venture, take one more pause. Maybe this is a day, a week, or a month, but stop and make sure you are completely confident you have everything covered. If after this pause, you're still a little hesitate, stop everything.

Until you have fully committed you can stop. Until you have signed the lease, the loan documents, hired employees, until any of those things have happened and cannot be undone, you can change your mind. Don't let embarrassment get in the way, if you're not sure, don't do it.

Never, ever think you will figure out what you don't know on the fly, not a smart move. Jumping into a new business venture with your eyes closed is not what you want to do. Back off, find a job; don't move forward just because that is what everyone is expecting. It is your responsibility to know if you have done all you can to create a successful business. If you're not sure stop.

If you know someone who owns their own business, go talk to them. Tell them your concerns, your fears and listen to what they say. Maybe they say you should do more work, sounds like you're not ready, then pay attention. If they say, it's normal to have cold feet, but you've done a great job preparing; you need to continue--then do it.

Now this may start to sound silly, but I encourage you to talk to your parents, older siblings, anyone you trust and lay-out what you are planning. You don't have to ask for advice from these people, more than likely they will willing give it—listen. These are people who want you to succeed, but also don't want you to fail. They may see the downside risk better than you—listen. I'm not saying don't do this if you don't get 100%, I'm just saying listen and learn. If they voice concerns, take those concerns to heart, and think about the risk.

Ultimately every new business owner will reach the point of knowing they have done all they can do and are ready to get started on their dream; that final decision is up to you. If you think you're ready, then you are.

10
Day One.

I know I said this book is not about check lists, but here is one. It is now Day One and soon you will be facing your worst and most crucial critic, a customer. Customers can be demanding, annoying, unrealistic, rude; but they are what it is all about. The customers decide if you are a success or a failure. Hate or love 'em, they are the most important piece of the puzzle. Are you ready?

This list is not all inclusive and remember each business will have some unique issues, requirements, needs that must be addressed. This is a general list of items that should be in place on Day One, many will not be because of this or that excuse, but the more of these that are ready on Day One the more likely you will experience success sooner rather than later.

- Employees. Do you have enough help? Are they trained? Has each employee completed all paperwork and training as needed? A bad employee can cost you your business, do not allow an unqualified employee to work in your business. If you are not comfortable with an employee deciding your fate, let that person go, before they deal with customers. Teach employees how to be successful, make sure you have given them the tools to succeed. Written material should be in place that tells each employee how to do their job.
- Data collection and record keeping. Are systems in place that will capture the information you will need to evaluate and adjust your business? This will cover revenue, costs, times, em-

ployee hours, every detail of your business needs systems in place to capture critical information. On Day One it should all have been tested and re-tested to make sure everything is working as needed.

- Store appearance and presentation. Before customers visit your business, have you done everything to have the correct appearance and proper presentation of your product or service? This is signage, layout, lighting, printed material everything that creates an impression on the customer.
- Pre-Opening promotions and marketing. You only get to open once, have you done the pre-opening promotions and marketing to announce the beginning of your business. Have you taken advantage of free exposure with news releases to local media?
- Web site up and ready. No matter your industry, you will need a web site. For some businesses this is a critical piece of your operations, for others this is mostly a marketing tool. Whatever category you are in, it must be up and running. Customers expect your business to be ready to go in all aspects once you open the doors. Test and retest all systems to make sure they are working properly.
- Loyalty and Membership programs are up and running. No matter how you interact with your customers you will want to know as much about them as possible. The best way to do that is a membership program with special benefits. Another is a loyalty program with special benefits.
- Special programs in place. Does your business require an app to be successful, if so, it should be in place and tested on Day One.
- Social Media. Announcing your business to the world will be a critical function of social media. Is your presence on these

platforms ready to go? Have plans been made for the first month of social media activity. Has someone been assigned those tasks?

- Practice. Just like in sports, practice is important to success when the game starts. Have you had trial runs, pretend customers, tested all systems with actual transactions? Practice, practice, and practice again before you open.
- All suppliers on board and supportive. Make sure all your suppliers know when you first day of business will be, ask them to be supportive in any way that makes sense.
- Professionals on board and supportive. Some businesses will have more professionals than others. But most all businesses should have an accountant/CPA and probably an attorney, and maybe even a banker. These people should be aware of Day One and ask them to be supportive.
- Are all needed licenses and permits in place. Obviously on Day One they should be. Make sure something in this area does not fall through the cracks.
- Policy and Procedure manuals in place? Some form of this should be available for all businesses. In some industries this can be a very large document in others not so much. But every business should write a set of policy and procedures that will be followed by all employees.
- Details on product preparation or service procedures. All material in this area should be written and reviewed with all relevant employees.
- Test runs. Everything that goes on in the business should be tested and retested before actual productions begins.
- Free media coverage. Where possible let local media know about the opening of the new business. All free media coverage is good.

- All operational equipment has been tested and checked to make sure it is in good working order.
- Safety and health protocols must be written and discussed with employees.
- Long term marketing and promotion programs are in place and ready to go.
- Security training for all employees has been completed. Certain training materials in this area are available to employees in written form.
- You are rested and ready to work harder than you ever have, yes?

Summary

You may think you have answered every question about your leap into entrepreneurship, but you haven't. Surprises will be the biggest challenge in a new business. You mitigate those challenges with planning and research. Test every assumption you have as best you can. Develop a business plan, not because it will ensure your success but because it is a good exercise that will help you in many ways you did not anticipate. Writing down you plans is better than just talking about them, the exercise itself will help create discipline.

There are no sure things in business. In most cases your path to success will be based on having a lot of money and luck. Lack of money is the number one reason businesses fail. It's not magic, money does allow you to fail but have the resources to correct your mistakes and try again and again.

The best business ideas are not always unique or revolutionary, often they are slight improvements to existing businesses that are succeeding. If your business idea is unique and original, be careful who you tell about it until you get iron-clad non-disclosure agreements signed.

If you think self-employment is going to be a cake walk, you should stick with your job and hope for a lottery win or a big inheritance. Self-employment will be one of the toughest things you have ever done, even if you succeed. It can be life changing for good or bad.

Never stop learning and improving whatever your business venture. Appreciate and properly value employees who in most cases are more important to your business than you are. Stay humble if you succeed and stay positive if you fail.

Enjoy the ride.

Running a Successful Small Business

1

Numbers to Know—Key Performance Indicators.

Key performance indicators (KPIs) refer **to a set of quantifiable measurements used to gauge a company's overall long-term performance**. KPIs specifically help figure out a company's strategic, financial, and operational achievements, especially compared to those of other businesses within the same sector. (Twin, 2021) (https://www.investopedia.com/terms/k/kpi.asp)

Now, what does that really mean? The most basic of these key measures might be revenue. For most businesses this is the most important number to know. What was revenue today compared to last year, or what has revenue averaged per hour for the last week. Other information might be sales per labor hour, or just cost of labor as a percentage of revenue.

Every business will have a set of KPI's that tells management what is happening in the business. It is important to set up what means the most to you as the owner, what do you want to see that will help you manage the day-to-day operations.

Let's look at some KPIs for a couple of industries.

Restaurants

1. Sales/Revenue. This can also include Break-Even sales point and Gross Profit percentage of revenue. There are many ways to look at sales, such as sales per sq.ft., sales per ticket, sales per customer, sales per employee. You will

be able to find industry norms for these types of measures so that you can compare your operation with a typical restaurant.

2. Historical Sales. Maintain extensive records on sales gives you the opportunity to measure your current sales to historical numbers to measure trends and find weaknesses and strengths. Often your accounting system will capture some of this, but you will need to look at other ways to capture and store some of this data.
3. Labor Costs. For a restaurant a good rule of thumb is labor costs of 30% to 35% of revenue. It's possible your niche in the industry is higher or lower—you should get this data from industry trade sources so you can measure your performance.
4. Cost of Goods. A normal percentage should run between 28% to 35%.
5. Prime Costs. This is the joint cost of labor and COGS. Typical restaurant would be 60% to 65%.
6. Employee Turn-over Rate. For small business this may not be that critical, in that you are there every day, and you know if turnover is out of hand. You care about turnover because every new employee costs you to train and if you are losing people after a short interval you will need to address what is causing that and how to fix it. Long-term employees almost always add value.
7. Server Benchmarks. If you have full service in your restaurant there are many benchmarks you will want to develop to measure the performance of your key staff.

Retail

1. Sales per Sq. Ft. This is an important measure that reduces the impact of store size when trying to compare different locations performance. This is also a measure that can rank you with top performers or bad performers in your industry.
2. Customer Satisfaction. One of the challenges here is how to measure. On-line reviews and ratings can help, many businesses do customer surveys. The better you can test this and understand the good or bad that shows up, the better you can manage your business.
3. Inventory Turnover.
4. Gross Profit Margin
5. Marketing as a Percentage of Sales.
6. Order Fulfillment Cycle Times.
7. Selling, General and Administrative (SG&A) costs as a percentage of Revenue.

Hopefully you can see that these measures can be extensive, complicated to accurately calculate and time consuming to analyze. Is it worth the effort? Yes. As you develop the systems to gather this data you will start to build you own KPI's that make sense to you. You are not just trying to find numbers that are good or bad, you are looking for trends. If revenues are declining most business owners can see that and try to do something about it. But often the problems are buried and not obvious. The right KPI's can give you a warning something is wrong before it becomes critical.

As an example, let's look at a small construction business, Joe's Fences. Joe mostly builds residential wood fences. He has a crew of 15 people, with a small office and yard where he stores fence material. Joe is the salesperson and spends much of his time responding to inquiries and giving bids. Joe also makes frequent stops at work sites and discusses problems or progress on the fence projects. There are a couple of people in the office who handle phone calls, bookkeeping, payroll, and paperwork. Joe's business is a cash basis business, he does not extend credit but does accept credit cards. He usually will secure at least 50% deposit on each project when the customer accepts the bid and the balance upon completion. What should Joe's KPIs be?

First, as with most businesses, is revenue. Joe's revenue numbers consist of completed jobs and work-in-progress. Some of Joe's jobs are larger commercial projects that can take weeks or longer to complete, therefore, it is important for him to know how much he has earned based on a percentage of completion report. Joe's cycle for this info is on a weekly basis, unlike retail or food services, he is not concerned with daily revenue numbers, nor does he value comparisons to last year-- except monthly.

So, for revenue Joe wants to see:

1. Revenue for completed Jobs. This is a weekly report.
2. Revenue for WIP for the week. This is a weekly report.
3. Monthly Revenue (completed and WIP) compared to last year.

All work is secured through bids and that information is critical to Joe.

4. Bids sent this week. This tracks number of bids and total dollars for the week
5. Bids outstanding this week. This report tracks bids sent to customers that are still open waiting for the customer

response.

Labor (excluding office labor) and material costs are Joe's biggest costs. He will want to check labor as a percentage of jobs.

6. Total direct labor costs as a percentage of revenue and WIP.
7. Direct labor costs as a percent of each job. This is important to Joe both as an on-going measure of profits but also to make sure his estimates of labor for bids are accurate. This requires Joe to have his workers track hours per job.
8. Material costs as a percentage of revenue and WIP.
9. Material costs as a percent of each job.

Those might be Joe's KIPs that he closely monitors. He would also have a monthly P&L and Balance Sheet that he would review, possibly with his accountant. If Joe was storing a significant inventory, he might want on-going reports detailing the total inventory by category and the turnover of that inventory.

Joe's KPIs are not locked in concrete. He may change them as he feels he needs to track something else. Or he may change some of the numbers to monthly not weekly items if there is not much week-to-week change. Joe decides what is critical to him and helps him the most in managing his business. Each business and business owner will be different and want different information. And there is a limit to how much of this you can use. It costs money to track things and that is a factor in deciding the worth of the data.

Financial statements give the owner the big picture of the business, but those numbers can be too late to stop trends quickly. The KPIs are a short-term quick snap shot of the most critical measures that you can use to track problems, pick up on trends and spot trouble. Every business owner, whether you're a small business or a big business, must manage the day-to-day operation mostly from numbers. If you're a small business and you work everyday firsthand, many things someone stuck in an office might want to see, you will see each day as you deal directly with the business. But don't fool yourself into thinking because you are working every day and see everything that you understand what the numbers are doing. Trust your eyes but pay attention to the quantifiable details that will decide success or failure.

If you're not sure what your industry's KPI's might be, then you should do research. You can find a lot on the internet. Trade associations can be helpful. There are books devoted to KPI's and how to find them and how to use them. Ask an accountant/CPA. Even ask other business owners in your industry what key numbers they use to manage their businesses. Some will not be helpful, but most will be generous with their time and knowledge.

The most important aspect of this is to understand that this is something you should do.

2
Budgeting.

"I don't want to become an accountant!" "Numbers, numbers, is that all you can think about?"

My background is financial, and I can understand if that is not your thing, the constant emphasis on this kind of stuff can be annoying. One thing to remember is that all these numbers are representative of money. It is money that I keep emphasizing. The numbers are your way of showing what is important in the pursuit of profits.

As a business owner your goal is profits. Without profits you cannot survive. Sure, there are the stories of big start-ups who have survived for years, if not decades, losing money. But they had something you probably don't; willing investors handing them millions of dollars. There are three sources of money to keep your business afloat, investors (thanks, Dad! —or even your own money), debt or profits. Most small businesses might have some access to investment money, but usually it is debt that supplements the owner's investment to keep everything running. The biggest problem with debt is that it has be paid back with interest. Also, a major drawback with debt is there must be someone willing to loan money to a struggling small business.

The most important source of funds to supply a small business the resources to survive and grow, is profits. Profits literally means survival. Without profits you will eventually go under.

As I have said in different contexts, planning is the best guarantee of success and profits. Budgeting, even on a small scale, is one of your best tools to understanding how all the pieces of your business fit together. Can you be a successful business owner without budgeting, of course. Do you personally have to prepare budgets to get the benefits, no. If you hate numbers, one of your first chores as a new business owner should be to find an accountant, or a "numbers" person who can help you with these tedious tasks.

If you have worked in big business, you know all about budgets. Almost every large company will have an extensive process to develop budgets on an annual basis. Some of this would have looked like a waste of time to you, but the budgets often have great importance to top management. They want to see what each piece, department, segment, division is budgeting and why. It is a form of communication. As a small business owner, you don't need a budget to communicate with yourself on what you think will happen in the future, but it is a good tool to quantify where you think the business will be in the next year or beyond.

Budgets are a good way to plan and think about the future. To put everything in black and white, numbers force a certain discipline that is not needed if you're just brainstorming.

I have often told small business owners that the best path to success is to mimic what big business does but don't do it in the stupid way they do. What that means is that big business will often keep doing things that don't really work because it has become a habit or part of the culture. All employees of big companies will tell you they waste an incredible amount of time doing something stupid, and often that can be budgets.

But those budgets, at least at one point in time, were a critical part of the success of that now big business. Maybe it has turned into a pointless exercise, but for small business I believe these practices of thinking and planning are a key to success.

Managing any business, small or large, is about understanding the numbers and having the numbers available to understand. Can you succeed by running your new small business by the seat of your pants? Yes, you can. There have been many success stories where the owner thought planning and numbers were evil forces sucking out his vital juices. Okay, should you follow that guy? No. The people who succeed without planning, without putting systems in place to secure numbers and understanding what those numbers are telling you, are lucky, not smart. So, if you want to bet your house, your savings, your family on luck, go for it.

My advice is to put together a detailed first year budget, this is by month for the first twelve months with even weekly breakdown of projected revenues. Also put together a couple of more years on an annual basis. That would give you a detailed first year and a total of three years on an annual basis. If this is a major hurdle and mind bogging to you, at least try for the first year by month. This is important to give you a benchmark to measure actual results against. Were your assumptions close to actual or miles apart. The quicker you can recognize the accuracy of your planning, the better you can adjust to deal with higher or lower numbers.

Another reason, as mentioned, now repeated, is that you will learn much about the detail of your business by preparing a budget and then measuring that against actual numbers. Successful small business owners must be learning every day, it's the only way to get better.

3
Employees.

Almost every business will need employees. Some might not need many, others will need a lot. This need is one that is most difficult to plan for and to evaluate. If you're a retail business, you will need inventory. That is easy to plan for and evaluate. If you're a food service business you're going to need more employees than you first thought. You need x number to work the hours you are open, but you will also need back-up employees, you will probably need part-time employees to fill-in if a regular is sick, you will need extra employees during busy times. How do you know how many you will need, how do you train these people to do exactly what you want, how do you ensure that each employee is honest and hardworking, where do you find these people? Employees for most business owners are their biggest headache.

During my days as a small business consultant the number one complaint about being a small business owner was employees. Often the tone of this conversation was very negative. The owner had reached the point in his business cycle where he blamed almost every problem on bad employees. Without looking at any financial data I knew the business was in trouble, or if it wasn't in trouble now, it would be shortly. If employees are a functioning part of your business and you think they are not doing the job and all you do is complain about it, you will soon not have a business, or employees, to worry about.

So, who is responsible here? Are all employees out to take advantage of small business owners and make their lives miserable?

Often, employees will say the worst employers are small business owners who don't know how to manage people. What is really going on?

Over the years I've seen some bad situations caused by lousy relations between the owner and his employees, I've also seen some model circumstances where the employees are considered the biggest asset of the business by the business owner. What makes that difference? In almost all cases it is ego. Your ego. If you only hire people who will say "yes, boss", you will not have hired the best people. In most cases your employees are your biggest asset, you should treat them that way.

If you can, hire people who know more than you do. Listen to them and learn. It is still your business so you can decide what is right and what is not, but don't turn off some of your best resources by acting like you know everything and don't need any advice. Everyone, from the smartest business owner to the dumbest needs advice. It's only the dumbest that don't take it.

In most cases you will be hiring people who may not know as much as you, then it is up to you to train them. Training and ongoing communication about the progress of employees is the best way for you to affect the ability of your employees to achieve the goals you set for them. Every employee in your business should be treated as an asset if you cannot do that, you might want to reconsider if self-employment is for you.

Now, of course, everyone makes employment mistakes. You hire someone who totally impressed you during the interview process. That person seemed the perfect fit, you congratulated yourself on a great hire. Within weeks (or days) it becomes obvious you made a mistake; it happens a lot in business.

Remember this book is about generalities, it covers all small businesses, therefore cannot be specific. But let's once again think about Bob's restaurant. He will be hiring kitchen staff, front counter people and clean-up people. Naturally Bob's priority for the front counter people would be customer relations, which is obvious. However, it's not a big priority for the dishwasher. Every business will have different requirements for different jobs. It's important to show what skills are needed and to detail the job responsibilities. Large companies go to an amazing effort to describe the job and the responsibilities associated with the job. Duties are described in detail. Should you do this, yes. Will you, probably not. But you should do some of it. You should let your new employees know what you considered important in their jobs, and if possible, to rank those qualities from highest to lowest.

Bob might put together a list like this for every employee, no matter the specific duties.

1. Customer relations. Every employee handles making the customer experience in our restaurant as pleasing as possible.
2. Health and Safety. Every employee handles maintaining the highest standards of cleanliness as set out in greater detail describing process and procedures for maintain a safe working environment and a sanitized operation.
3. Promotion support. I expect every employee to promote the business as best they can to existing and future customers. This is the business that supplies our income. If you cannot be positive and encourage people to visit this restaurant you should not work here.
4. Workplace communications. Confrontation with coworkers will not be tolerated. Any conflict during working hours is my business. Bring all such matters to my attention at once.

5. Punctuality and dependability. Everyone is expected to be at work and ready to work at your scheduled time, not five minutes late. If you are late, you are affecting co-workers, and this will not be tolerated. Absences for health will be excused with proper communication.
6. Work performance and reviews. Everyone will receive a regular scheduled work performance review. During this review you will be advised if your work is not satisfactory and ways you can improve your job performance. At any time, if you feel you have not received adequate training to do your job, you should let me know. It is your responsibility to understand what is expected of you in this job and if you think you lack the proper tools to complete your job successfully, you must tell me, so that I can help you achieve success.
7. Theft and waste. Stealing, even small items, will not be tolerated. This is a firing offense without notice. Please understand this is a business where pennies matter. It is very important for our success that we watch all costs very closely, this is part of your job no matter what function you are fulfilling.
8. Appearance. Every employee should be prepared to meet the public and be groomed and dressed in a proper manner. Even backroom jobs may require you to interact with the public and you should be prepared to do that. We have specific dress standards that you have been given and it's your responsibility to meet those standards.
9. Complaints and grievances. Any issues with your job or co-workers should be brought to my attention. No matter the issue you should give me the opportunity to be involved in resolving any problems to make this the best

workplace possible. I guarantee you that I will listen and try to make corrections if needed.

10. Firings. Sometimes things don't work out. This is going to be my fault, more than yours. If this results, we will talk about it, and I will help you as best I can to understand why this has happened. I want you to succeed at Bob's but if you don't, I'm as much at fault as you.

As a small business owner, you will spend a significant amount of time dealing with employee issues. You will not have a human resources department; it will be you. The better you are at communicating to your employees what you expect the greater the chance they will do what you want. Most employees want to succeed at their job, yes, even the dishwasher. Treat every job in your business as important because it is.

In Bob's case, he might have the general list as we saw above, he also would have specific job descriptions for each job in his business. In his case he would detail the responsibilities of the front counter people, the kitchen staff, and the cleaning positions. He would go over those details and update them as needed. These are not 'one and done' documents, they are constantly being updated and improved to make it easier for the next employee to understand what is expected.

All of this is time consuming. It is easy to just wing it and see what happens, and many small business owners will take that approach. If you want to improve your chances of success, this is an area where there is great opportunity to make your employees better from day one, and that makes your business and you better from day one.

4

Managing Assets.

Assets are normally identified as tangible and intangible. A tangible asset might be physical things, such as inventory, trucks, employees, cash, accounts receivables, customers list, while intangible is non-physical, such as reputation, brand, patents, trade secrets, apps, web sites and on and on. Some of these can be both tangible and intangible, but all assets are the responsibility of the business owner to protect and manage.

Things that are physical, such as inventory or vehicles, are easy to recognize as assets and there are responsibilities in supporting and protecting those assets. Intangible assets can be a little vague in terms of value and what should be done to protect that value.

One source of recognizing these assets is a balance sheet. This is an accounting report that lists assets and liabilities and the net worth of the business. The net worth is the value of assets minus the amount of debt. A balance sheet can give you a picture of a business but in many cases, it is a false picture. One example, your most valuable asset might be your employees, they are not listed on a balance sheet.

Only items that have been quantified, usually by buying them, go on a balance sheet. So, most intangible assets would not go onto the balance sheet. Such as the value of a web site. You might have spent $5,000 in costs to develop your web site which shows up on the balance sheet (or doesn't if that amount was expensed as current period costs). While the web site might be the engine that drives all business transactions and worth hundreds of times more than the actual sunk cost.

Or another intangible asset could be your brand, company name, logo or even reputation could be included in the value of a brand. Almost none of that would be listed on a balance sheet. Accounting has rigid ideas about what should and shouldn't be put on a balance sheet, it's not all inclusive, but better than nothing. I think in many ways accounting has not kept up with the changing technology world in terms of assets and how to quantify them.

In an operating business the best way to find the value of assets is to have an appraisal done on the business. This would be a business valuation. This process looks at the value of the operating business including goodwill. Goodwill will often stand for the value of the intangibles associated with customers, brands, logos, and other non-quantified assets. I've written a book "How to Sell Your Business Without a Broker", where I go into great detail on how to calculate the value of a business. These are things, as a business owner, you should understand for your type of business.

The easiest way to get a sense of value is to find a rule-of-thumb valuation formula for your type of business. These are simplified ballpark estimates that can give you a best guess at a value. Keep in mind a real valuation will be much more complicated and correct as opposed to this "back of the envelope" approach, but with that said, the rule-of-thumb will be useful information. These are often multiples of something that is easily found in that business. Such as a multiple of annual revenues, or a multiple of earnings, or owners' discretionary income. There are books available that will give you a rule of thumb for your industry. Or you can usually contact a trade association and they will have this type of data. Almost all industries will fit into an overall model of 4 to 6 times Earnings Before Interest, Taxes, Depreciation and Amortization

(EBITDA). Remember all these rule-of-thumbs measures or the typical EBITDA multiples are estimates. The value of any business can be completely different due to unique circumstances with that business. The only way to know the value of a specific operating business is to have a business valuation done by a professional.

But the estimates have value. As an example, let's say a business is generating $100,000 in annual EBITDA, the value of that company might be $400,000. The book value of that same business, assets minus liabilities (all these rules of thumb or standard EBITDA multiples assume the value is for a debt free business) might be $300,000. That would mean that business has a goodwill of $100,000. That could be also stated as the value of intangible assets.

Protecting those intangible assets is often more important than maintaining tangible assets. This may require legal protection, such as patents, trademarks, copyrights, and other legal means to protect your ownership of those assets. Or human assets might need to be protected with employment agreements, or non-compete agreements, non-disclosure agreements or other legal documents.

When a small business starts most of these things about protecting assets are not a priority. But I wanted to include this chapter to emphasize that as you grow and reach success you will need to be aware of these requirements and how they can affect the next level of your business success.

5

Marketing and Promotion.

If no one knows about your new business, it could be lonely. Some businesses can open with a bang without much hoopla, but most need to make noise to get noticed. An example of opening advantage is the restaurant industry. People pay attention to new restaurants and often are eager to give them a try. The problem with that is they may try you at your worst and never come back. If you're a repair service business more than likely you will start slow, and have time to get your act together, before you experience a high volume of customers.

Each business is different, but most will need to do marketing and or promotion to get the ball rolling. We will discuss what that might look like later. First let's emphasize my point above. You need to be ready for business before you toot your horn. Like I said some businesses don't have much choice they better be ready from day one, restaurants and some retails are the best examples. If this is your fourth restaurant, no problem; if it's your first—not so easy.

As you might expect based on the things I have already discussed, my recommendation is that you build a marketing/promotional plan. Before you open you should have developed a detailed plan on how you are going to spend you budgeted money for these areas. If this is just mind boggling, then hire someone who knows your industry to help you develop this plan. Once again, money rears its ugly head. If you don't have the resources to hire someone, give it a try but keep your budget small. Trial and error can be effective learning techniques but be cautious with those bucks. Spending advertising dollars on something that does not work is like burning money.

I have worked with small businesspeople who were spending thousands of dollars per month and getting poor results but would say they could not afford to hire someone to help them. What they cannot afford is wasting money on something that doesn't work, that is the double whammy. An axiom that might fit here is if you don't know what you're doing, don't do it.

Another odd phenomenon in advertising is that you're too successful. Yep, it happens. You budget X and it generates three times the responses you were expecting. Yippee! Well, maybe? You didn't have that much product. Your crews can't get to that much work in months? Calls mean bids and it will take you weeks to meet all these people, and they won't wait. Yes, this can be a problem, if you're not ready for the demand that your promotions might generate. Like I said this is an unusual problem, but it can happen. This can happen when you are just throwing money at promotion without a good understanding of the expected results. The downside to this is that you can alienate customers. You just ran ads saying you had the latest best seller for only $1, but you only had twenty and fifty people showed up to buy. Understanding advertising and promotions is also understanding what to expect. That knowledge is usually gained with experience. If you don't have that experience in this area, try to find someone who does, it will help you in the long run—might even cost you less than if you're handling everything yourself.

There are many other areas of promotion and advertising that you or your employees may be able to handle. Such as in store promotions, loyalty programs, direct communications, web site, social media; all of these will be an important part of your overall advertising plan.

As you're hiring people, you might want to ask them if they are active on social media and if they would be interested in setting up the company's social media sites. The person you were considering for the back-office function may turn out to be a wizard in that world.

Many small businesses do not contact local media sources. Sending out a press release may feel foreign to you, but with just a little Google search you find templates that you can copy. This may generate nothing, but it costs you almost nothing. And if you can get an interview with a local newspaper about your new business, it can be like finding gold.

6
Being Visible.

As we discussed in the earlier chapter you will need to run up the flag with advertising and promotion to let customers know about your business. Grand opening specials, meet and greets with key customers, social media splashes, web site announcements and specials; all sorts of things go on to get your business started on a good path to success. One that is often overlooked in our connected world is your community.

In many smaller communities, businesspeople are still very much the backbone of the community. Even in larger cities, your local community maybe only a few blocks but often will have its own network of important and influential citizens. This process of making connections can be time consuming and maybe not something the business owner is interested in pursuing, but it will have beneficial impact if you take the time to meet and greet these people. Also, there are often local civic groups that can have a real influence in the success of your business. It would be best to find out about these groups and make connections.

Is this the most important step in your operational plan, probably not; but it can be a benefit to get involved in your local community both for your business and for yourself. If you spend all your time with your employees, you can lose perspective and miss good input from people who are not working for you. Reach out and find other businesspeople who you can share some of the burden you will have in common. I have also found that other businesspeople will some of your greatest cheer leaders; they sincerely want to see you succeed, often because of their own self-interest. A successful community enhances their chances for success.

Visibility is getting to know your community, the schools, the churches, the organizations, the government agencies, the police, the fire department—every aspect of your community is an opportunity to be more visible. Join groups, join non-profit support groups, join civic groups—the more involved you are the better the community will support you. As an employee you can just work and go home, as a business owner in your community you should do more, be more engaged, be more concerned—be involved.

Many business owners will say they don't have time, but my experience suggests that if you don't take time to find other avenues for you to support your community and your business you will go nuts. You need to meet other business owners and talk about the bigger picture of what is good for business in general and not always just look at what is good for you. I really believe this helps in your success path.

Another area of engagement that I strongly suggest is trade associations. These exist for almost all types of business. This is a great source of data and usually will offer opportunities to participate in local and even national programs that will expand your knowledge and increase your visibility.

7

Break-Even Analysis.

If your new business did \$50,000 its first month did you make money, lose money or break-even. You should know the answer to that before you get a P&L statement. Understanding your break-even is a basic bit of financial analysis that every businessperson needs to be comfortable with. What does it mean? It's simple, you didn't make money, nor did you lose money.

The basic formula is revenue less fixed costs minus variable costs equals break-even.

Example

A service company run by the owner without employees. Fixed costs are rent, utilities, truck expense, telephone, and insurance. Variable expenses are permits, gasoline, part-time help, and materials.

Fixed expense	= \$2250
Variable expense	= 20% of revenue
Break-even sales	= x

Calculate x:

$$x = \$2250 + 0.20x$$

$$.80x = \$2250$$

$$x = \$2812$$

Proof:

Sales	$2812
Expenses:	
Fixed	$2250
Variable	$562
Total Exp.	$2812

This is of course a very simple model which can be found in the Appendix of this book titled Easy Accounting.

As you can imagine this can become very complicated. Expenses/costs can be both fixed and variable. A certain expense might be fixed up to a certain amount of revenue (such as rent) and then variable over that amount (rent paid as a percentage of sales after a certain fixed level). You could have labor that was fixed but based on certain performance criteria includes a bonus. All of that is probably left to someone comfortable man-handling numbers. The basic concept of understanding relationship with certain costs is critical knowledge for any business owner.

What you should know as an owner is the relationship of numbers and how it affects your opportunity to make a profit. Back to the food business. You might be working with a variable food cost of 30% and based on that you have calculated your break even at a certain number. So, you reach that sales number, and you get a P&L that shows you lost money—what happened? Your food costs were 35% and at that number you would have to increase your revenues substantially to overcome that higher food costs. Now you must go to work, is that an exception and it will come down next month, does it stand for higher waste due to employees not managing food prep, is someone stealing food, is it due to poor portion control? All of those and other options will have to be examined at once to figure out what is going on? Maybe you have priced your product incorrectly. You made certain assumptions when you developed prices, but did something change? Should you raise prices?

What this tells you is that you have work to do. Everything must be examined and analyzed. You can't increase prices, which will have a negative impact on sales, for any month where the numbers are not right and then lower them the next month because the numbers are better, your customers will be confused and, more than likely, you will lose business. On the other hand, you cannot run at a loss.

These numbers may tell you that you need tighter control over food prep related to portions, you might need to review buying practices to make sure all your original assumptions about price are still valid, waste can be accidental or poor training or theft—what is it?

We're using a restaurant as an example, but any business will have some similar issues. Inventory is the most dramatic loss control item in retail. Your cost of goods sold could skyrocket if you are not controlling inventory. This is a security issue related to theft, by employees or customers. This is a purchasing issue if the inventory is not being properly checked into the stores systems.

The better understanding the business owner has of a break-even analysis and a good handle on all the moving parts, the better the owner can track down problems and fix them.

8
Cash vs. Accrual Accounting.

Here we go again with accounting gobbledygook. Who cares about accounting anyway? You should. What is accounting? It is a system that has certain standard rules that give you, the owner, the best tool you will have to manage your business. Many hands-on owners do not believe that statement. I'm there every day and I know what is going on, okay, maybe. The real bugaboo about accounting is that your accounting system is a mess and the information you're getting from it is garbage.

Those reports based on your very flawed accounting system is useless and should be ignored, so is that a good reason to reject all accounting data as useless? That would be silly. If you are going to have bad accounting systems and let it stay that way, then accounting will not help you run your business. Now maybe, you would say, good, I hate accounting. That is bad business. Do big companies spend a ton of money on accounting, you better believe it. Is that because the CEO of Big Biz, Inc. is an accountant and he just loves numbers, hell, no. It's because that is the only way that CEO can tell what is going on with his vast enterprise.

A small business owner can say I can see all my operations right here and I know what is happening. That statement can be true, but in most cases, it is just a myth the owner has developed that he knows what is happening. He can see the theft of critical supplies that occurs at night, he can't see the flawed invoicing that is not properly billing the customers. The best way for the owner to have a handle on his business is through numbers—his accounting system.

There is some discussion of accounting systems in the appendix, but this book's scope can't begin to cover the right accounting software for your firm or how to make it work for you. I will say I have used QuickBooks for small business and for medium sized business and it works. Do others work, sure. It's accounting and the rules are the same. The most critical part of the accounting system is the business owner, if the owner thinks it's a waste of time to emphasize the need for good accounting, then his employees will ignore all the accounting requirements to secure good data, and everything will be garbage. If the owner says this is the most critical source for information about the health of my business and you will follow all rules put in place to get good numbers, then it will happen. I would like to preach some more about the importance of a good accounting system and the employees or outside skill people to make it work, but I will move on now—but let me say once more this is as critical as anything you do as a business owner to ensure your success—invest in a good accounting system and the people to make it work.

One aspect of accounting that I think most small business owners do not completely understand is the difference between cash and accrual accounting. Conceptually, a business owner can understand cash accounting. You count revenue as cash received and you deduct expenses when they are paid. Easy. I took in $500 today and paid out $300, I made $200. Easy, I must be a CPA!

Now you have a truck payment you make at the first of the month, you have insurance you pay quarterly, you have some maintenance cost you pay when something breaks, you have a new AC unit you just put in the office which you paid in full, you have rent you pay once a month—along with other expenses occurring irregularly. So did you really make $200, of course not. Common sense says all those other costs need to be distributed to figure out profit or loss.

Accrual accounting attempts to meet one of the basic accounting standards, the matching of revenue with expenses for any period. If you had an annual insurance payment you made in January, accrual accounting would expense 1/12 of that expense each month. Or if you buy a truck, it would not be fully expensed the day you bought it but set up as an asset and the expense distributed each month based on the life of the truck. So, a truck with a cost of $25,000 and a salvage value of $5,000 and a useful life of years would be allocated each month at $416.66, expensing the entire net cost of $20,000 distributed over 48 months. An even better method would be to distribute the cost based on the actual use as measure by mileage.

The point of accrual accounting is the match the revenue earned with the cost associated with earning that revenue. The purpose is to give a more exact picture of what the business has "really" earned, not what cash was collected minus what was disbursed.

The only accounting system that has value to a business owner is the accrual accounting system. Cash basis may supply a method to do taxes which might be in the owner's benefit, but cash-based accounting does not give you any exact operational information you can use to manage the business.

Another area of accounting that is less likely to come into play in a small business but is just as important, is cost accounting. Cost accounting will be the systems used on manufacturing (which can include food service). This set of rules is trying to capture all elements that go into a product. If you were a small furniture manufacture, you would want to use cost accounting to make sure you're pricing your product profitability. You know the cost of wood, but how about overhead, how much of that should be included in each table?

I know I am repeating myself, but accounting is just a tool. If you take the time (and spend the money) to understand this tool, it will help you be a better businessperson and will increase your chances of being successful.

9 Understanding Your Customer and Your Competition.

You would think every business owner could tell you who their customers are and who the competition is. But often they cannot. Ask a business owner who is their target customer, they might say whoever walks in the door. There are businesses whose customer base is the general public, say a grocery store. But even then, most grocery stores would appeal to a certain part of the public, or their customers could be identified by location, such as within two miles of the store, or by income levels. If you say your customer is everybody, you are saying you don't know who your customer is. You should find out.

Knowing who is your most likely customer gives you all sorts of useful data. If you can say my customers are parents, with income above X, both are employed, both are readers, both share a love of skiing, they employ a babysitter, have two dogs, one works from home, the other commutes 40-mile round trip. Wow, how would you know all of that. Yes, that is the challenge, getting all that data. But just think, if you knew that much about each potential customer. You could focus all marketing to match your customer, you could tailor your product to those customers. Knowing as much as you can about your customer is another key to running a successful business.

One of the important tools in business is to build a database of your customers. Over time this can become one of your most valuable assets. Depending on your industry you can accelerate this data gathering process with loyalty cards, membership programs, special discounts to known customers and many other ways. Build a social media environment that will seek your customer, by targeting their interests. Create an interactive web site and try to engage your customers. Knowing your customer can give your insight into how to serve them better, along with a much improved approach to reaching key segments of the population who would be most likely to patronize your business.

Every business, every industry will be different in how they approach understanding and reaching their customers. The first step in that process is understanding who your target market is. Find all characteristics of your ideal customer and structure your business and your marketing to reach that customer.

Another area of knowledge that you need to develop and to constantly update, is your competition. No business exists in a vacuum. Your competition is not the enemy, but you should be aware of everything they are doing. Most of that is to just be aware of the obvious, such as pricing, marketing, product development, anything that is readily available to the public. I'm not suggesting spying, I'm just saying be aware.

Especially with retail and food service, paying attention to your competition is critical. Your customers can be loyal, but there are frequenting your competition, you need to know what your customers are seeing and how you stack up against that competition.

I've often recommended to certain types of businesses that they keep a regular schedule of shopping their competition. This also means keeping a data base of information gathered, prices, new products, special promotions, appearance, customer service, anything that can be useful to you to measure against what you are doing.

Something else that many business owners do not do, is meet

your competition. If there is a trade association within your industry, join and attend meetings. If your industry has stores, drop in and introduce yourself to the owner. Nobody is giving you trade secrets, but these people have more in common with you than almost anyone else. Even if you're in direct competition, it does not have to be ugly. Might surprise you how much you have in common.

10
Measuring Profits.

Yes, we are at the last chapter and what do I want to close with, accounting. Yuk! I understand this is not a fun subject. This book is about being successful in a small business, and what is the number one reason some businesses fail, and others succeed, well it's not accounting. As I've said before, it is money and luck—I know that is two number one reasons. Close behind money and luck is good financial records. Most small businesses cannot afford an accountant and for sure cannot afford a controller or heaven forbid a CFO. Big business spends incredible amounts of resources gathering and analyzing data, small businesses do not. That is a mistake. Of course, a small business cannot spend the money big guys do, but it is just as critical to a small business, or maybe even more so, to have good data to study and use to improve the financial performance of those businesses.

What I have seen in many small businesses is not a lack of resources to gather proper data, but business owners who think that the data, if gathered, would be useless. This is usually because that owner has tried to put in place an accounting system that gave him good performance information, he could use to manage his business and all he got was garbage. Many small businesses owners will buy accounting software and expect instant good data, but they only get muddled and inaccurate information because they do not put in place all the procedures and controls needed to be able to capture exact and useful information.

In the first chapter I told you this was a conversation about success, it was not a check list of how to do all the things you need to do to run a business, because each business will be somewhat different in the details. My goal was to lay out the major items that drive success. Good record keeping is one of them. How you do that, especially if it is not something you know much about, will be a challenge. More than likely, you will need help. Spending money on accounting is not something most small business owners want to do, but it is important.

Find an accountant, or bookkeeper to help you. You don't have to hire top dollar CPAs, just someone who understands the basics of accounting and how to implement the procedures to gather the data so you can manage the numbers. Discuss with this accountant the needs of your business. Think about the KPI's we have already gone over. Which ones of those are most important to your business? Ask for suggestions from the accountant.

You can find books about accounting, which will give you a detailed overview of accounting systems. You will also be able to find books for various specific industries, such as the restaurant industry. I reviewed two that I thought offered good advice, Accounting for Small Business Owners by Tycho Press and QuickBooks for Restaurants by Zachary Weiner. That's two of hundreds. If this is an area where you lack the skills that makes it the critical area to seek assistance.

There is no question, luck is a big factor in buildings a successful small business, but if you want to maximize your chances at success and not depend on just luck, accounting is that edge that can push you into the success path faster than anything else.

Believe me I am not suggesting that you become an accountant, if that is not the business you are in, then taking on the accounting job in your business is a serious mistake. I want you to become the analysist, who uses numbers to make good business decisions. I want you to be the boss who looks at the weekly KPI reports and see trends that are not good and fixes the issues. I want you to be the smart small business owner who can talk about your profitability in ways that show you understand all the elements of being successful. I want you to succeed and to know why you succeeded was not just random luck. Of course, having good luck is still a very good thing.

Another point about accounting and records, you should pay close attention to what is needed in your industry to meet all government regulations. Now this may sound lame to you, but this is critical. There are many requirements that must be met if you have employees, don't shrug that off and think nobody cares about my small business. It only takes one disgruntled employee to cause you grief if you are not following the rules. It is a lot easier to just follow the rules.

There are other areas where regulators have some control over most businesses, as simple as collecting sales tax and filing the proper and prompt reports. As a small business owner, you have the responsibility to know what is needed and put in place systems that will allow you to meet every requirement.

Now some of you may be rebels and will not do what is needed, trust me that is stupid. If you build your business on cutting corners, under the table deals, poor records, or make-believe accounting; you're building a business as a house of cards. One phone call from the labor department could mean the end of your business, or a tax audit, or an employee complaint about non-compliance for overtime. Don't do those things, follow the rules. If you need help understanding the compliance, then get it. Don't pretend you know everything, if you don't know how to do something, find someone who does and pay them to do it.

Sorry, I will stop preaching. My message, in general, is that accounting is the engine that keeps everything running smoothly. Information and data are the tools that makes you a smarter business owner. Success for most small businesses is built around good, reliable information. Don't think, just because you are working in your business every day, you know everything that is going on. The numbers might tell you a different story.

We began this book with me saying it would be a conversation between me and you, the small business owner. I wanted to offer you my experience and observation of many years in the small business world and show areas that will matter to your success.

For you to achieve your dream of a successful small business, you will work harder than you have ever worked for someone else, the hours will be longer, the stress greater; but the rewards will be larger. Success will almost be guaranteed if you have tons of money in the bank, because that cash allows you to fail and try again. Also, luck is an important factor that you cannot influence. Hard work will pay off, but it is always more than hard work. You must be smart in how you run your business. Smart business owners gather the information and data about their business and manage based on those numbers. Smart business owner's employ people with more skills than they have, and don't let their ego get in the way of listening to those employees. Successful employees will lead to a successful business.

Smart business owners plan and rethink every aspect of their business model, analyze and continuously self-correct. Business plans, budgets, marketing plans, policy and procedures, detail job descriptions and more are all tools to reach your goals. Follow the lead of big business, they don't do all the things they do just because they love detail work—it's because it works.

Never, ever be afraid to say you don't know. If you don't know, don't guess. Find someone who does know, hire them to help you. Just because you're the boss does not mean you are infallible, know your strengths and employ them, but also know your weaknesses and hire others to offer help in those areas. Every successful business is a team success. Recognize that and use the strengths of others to help you achieve your dreams.

2-for-1 Bonus:

easyAccounting

Chapter One

Importance of Good Records

Before we begin let me clarify, accounting is not easy. It's a catchy title but let's be honest, accounting is hard. Why is it hard. Mostly because it is a set of rules that must be followed to the letter, that most people don't know. It's not a secret but most businesspeople don't go to the effort to learn those rules. So, when confronted with accounting questions the best answer for most is to say something along the lines of "ask the accountant."

The small business owner usually doesn't have a full-time accountant that can be asked, so often accounting becomes a chore driven mostly by needed tax information, sales, or income tax data to fill out forms. I'm a financial person so my bias is towards the numbers as the biggest key to success in a small business, but if you ask businesspeople who have succeeded, many of them will tell you the first thing you need to do is *understand accounting.*

That's what we are going to do here, in a few chapters we will cover some of the basics and toss out some phrases, terms and calculations that a good business owner should become familiar with if they want to succeed.

Is accounting necessary to having a successful business, no. Does accounting help lead to success, yes. A good accounting system will provide you with information, data that you will need.

1. **How is your business doing financially?** That is what accounting does, it gives you the black and white answers to that question. To get accurate answers will not be easy but once you have your system in place the information can become automatic and the data invaluable.

2. **Real data will support your decisions.** Every business owner will make decisions every day about running their business. Are prices correct? Is my payroll to high? Should I reduce my hours of operation? The accounting system is meant to give you the actual data to make these and hundreds of other decisions. Accounting is not just tax reports and mundane useless numbers, it should be a critical picture of how your business is doing. That makes you a better manager of your business, real data will support good decisions.
3. **Borrowing Money.** What is the first thing a banker might ask for to evaluate a loan request, your financial statements. Sure, you could say you don't believe in such nonsense, but your loan request won't go far if you don't have financial reports. Many lenders will review financial statements to determine if they are interested in loaning you money, but also will use those reports as indicators that you are operating a professionally ran company.
4. **Other Sources of Capital.** Looking for investors, partners; someone to join your business and provide additional capital. Yep, first thing they will want to see is financial statements-if you are an operating business. If you don't have those that makes a bad statement. If you are saying how great you're doing but can't provide statements to back that up, most people will walk away holding their money tight.
5. **Budgeting.** Some people hate budgets, I love them. Yes, I know I have problems. Even if you hate budgets you need to developed detail budgets for your business. Why, you ask. Because it is a vital tool to help you succeed. Budgets are just a plan that you develop based on your best esti-

mates. You than should compare that plan to actual data. This will help you pinpoint areas of concern. Also, this process creates a better understanding of accounting.

6. **Tax Returns.** Now maybe you're one of those anti-tax people and never file a return, well forget accounting, and contact a good lawyer. If you file returns accounting is the source of all that data. Accounting also functions as a planning vehicle for you or a tax planner to take advantage of the numerous quirks in the tax laws that might help you lower your tax bill.
7. **Payroll Tax Rules**. Speaking of rules there are many government-imposed rules related to payroll. If you have employees, you will need to be able to demonstrate that you follow those rules. These rules run from overtime pay requirements to when and how you deposit payroll taxes. Your required to file regular payroll reports and provided W-2's to your employees. This is an area where you could face severe penalties if everything is not done timely. The only way to accomplish most of these tasks is with accurate and timely records.
8. **Sales Taxes**. If you collect sales tax, you can't keep it, I know, too bad. You must file detail reports, sometimes depending on your type of business and number of locations this can be quite complicated. Accounting systems are needed to support these files and to provide the detail records in case of an audit. Yes, sales tax audits do happen.
9. **Sharing the Wealth**. If you have partners or investors there may come a time when profits justified a distribution of profits. Accounting systems are the source for this data. If you're a corporation this maybe dividends, which once again will be based on profits determined by

accounting. I suppose you could just ballpark something but that would not be wise. Even friends or family members can be rather troublesome if they think they are not receiving their fair share. It is accounting statements that provide the basis to alleviate any concerns.

10. **Cashing In.** Your dream might be to sell your business for a huge pile of money. That dream will only happen if you are keeping good records. No one buys a business larger than a lemonade stand without seeing the "numbers". And those numbers must be supported, with audited statements or subject to detailed review. Many business buyers will decide about whether than think a business is managed well based on the reliability of the financial statement. It's hard to sell a pig in a poke.

Analyzing Your Financial Position

We will discuss the basics of accounting in just a little bit, but first, let's consider why you're doing all this hard work building an accounting system. Many new business owners are familiar with financial statements, such as Income Statement or a Balance Sheet. They probably could not "read" those statements and tell you what they mean, but they are familiar with those names.

Having data available from the accounting system allows you to use other tools to measure your business' financial performance. Business Ratios gives you a way to measure certain elements of your business against industry norms or budgets.

The Accounting System

Accounting is how financial information is gathered, processed, and summarized into reports based on a set of rules, established by the accounting profession's regulatory bodies. GAAP or General Accepted Accounting Practices is that set of rules.

Accounting today is done on computers using software that mimics the now outdated hand-posted double-entry system involving ledgers and journals. To understand accounting, you must have a basic understanding of how these ledgers and journals once worked.

Every accounting entry is based on a business transaction, those transactions generally will have documents to support the transaction. Those documents can be numerous and varied, typical docs would be a check or a sales invoice.

A journal, at one time these were actual books, is a place to record the transactions of a business. **Sales journal, cash receipts journals** and a **cash disbursements journal** are the most common journals. Closing each accounting period will often require special adjusting entries into the **general journal**.

All transactions are recorded into a journal as they happen. The **general ledger** contains all balance sheet, income, and expense accounts of the business.

A listing of all general ledger accounts is prepared with their balances, which is called a **trial balance**. The debit balances should equal the sum of the credit balances unless an error has been made. If these accounts don't balance, there have to be an analysis to find the mistake.

Using the data from a trial balance financial statements are prepared.

In automated systems most of these postings are done "behind the scenes", but the same process as was once done by hand in posting to these journals and ledgers goes on in an automated double entry bookkeeping system.

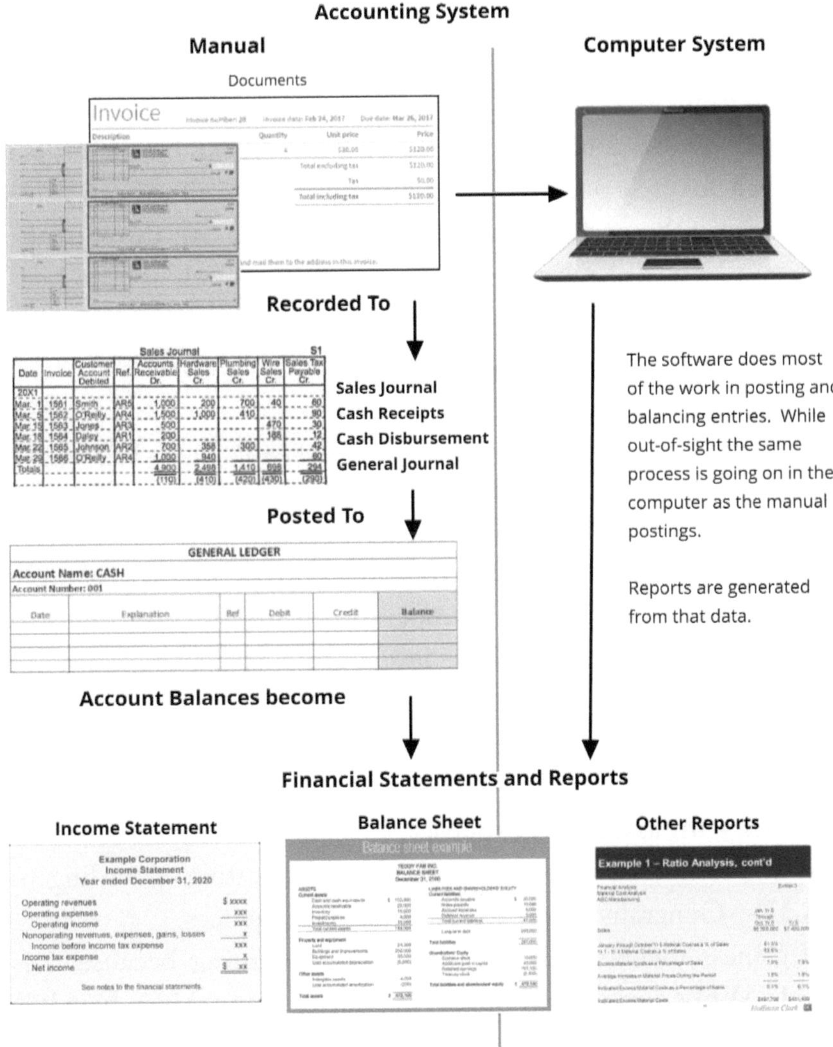

Chapter Two
Cash vs. Accrual Accounting

Most for-profit businesses will use either cash or accrual accounting. Both approaches record transactions; however only one has any real value to a business owner. The cash system of accounting is mostly used as a basis to file tax returns and can be the proper approach for that purpose. Cash accounting has almost no value for tracking the performance of a business. You can think of the cash system as a check register. We will discuss both approaches.

Cash accounting.

As I said cash accounting amounts to a check register. You record expenses when you write a check and record income when you make a deposit for work done. The obvious problem with this approach is that much of what you want from accounting is more than your bank balance—it is operational information that can penpoint financial performance levels. Cash accounting does not do this.

One of the basic principles in accounting is called the matching principle. This states that the objective of accounting is to match revenues with associated expenses. Cash accounting does not do that and is not an accepted method of accounting according to GAAP—Generally Accepted Accounting Practices.

Business owners will still use cash accounting because it is simple. While simple may have real value in many things here it is just not doing much and therefore it's simple, but almost useless.

Accrual accounting.

In accrual accounting you recognize income when it is earned and expenses when they are incurred. Accrual accounting goes to great lengths to match income and expenses. This is the GAAP accounting method for most businesses.

The critical distinction is timing. With the cash method everything centers around cash—while accrual accounting attempts to record all revenue and expenses based on accurate timing and when they were earned or the obligation to pay occurred.

An example might be insurance. Many businesses would pay their insurance once a quarter or even annually. If you paid your insurance in January for the year; cash accounting would show all of that expense as a January expense, when in reality the expense should be reflected 1/12 of the total each month of the year. Or if a contractor had a large job that took two months to complete and was paid upon completion. He would have expenses for many months but only show income for one—if using the cash method. The accrual method would show income as work progressed and allocate for that time frame—not only when money was received.

This takes extra effort to adjust expenses and revenues so that they match within the period they were earned or occurred. This extra effort is often the reason accounting systems become inaccurate. If someone is not handling these adjustments than the accrual system will end up being more of a cash system, with all the inherit inaccuracies.

There are IRS regulations about what businesses can use cash or accrual and rules about changing methods. But the most important aspect of using only accrual accounting it the usefulness of the financial information. If you accounting systems do not reflect a matching of revenue and expenses the resulting financial reports will be of no value in doing any analysis of the financial performance of the business. It will be the ultimate example of garbage in and garbage out.

Example A

Transactions during the month:

1. Completed $500 worth of services on credit.
2. Collected $250 from previous months customer
3. Completed $500 worth of services for cash
4. Paid for 6-month insurance premium. Cost was $600.
5. Paid truck payment of $400. Interest portion of payment was $100. Truck's original cost was $6000 and the truck had a useful life of 5 years.

	Cash Basis		**Accrual Accounting**
Revenue	$750		$1,000
Expenses			
Insurance	$600		$100
Truck	$400	Interest	$100
		Depr.	$100
Total Expenses	$1,000		$300
Profit or (Loss)	($250)		$700

Example B

Transactions during the month:

1. Sold $2,000 worth of material purchased last month for $1,500.
2. Collected $500 from previous months work.
3. Paid $1,000 worth of bills, covering two months expenses.

	Cash Basis	Accrual Accounting
Revenue	$2,500	$2,000
Cost of Goods Sold		$1,500
Gross Profit	$2,500	$500
Expenses	$1,000	$500
Profit or (Loss)	$1,500	$0

These examples show us how much difference there can be in Profit and Loss depending on the method used for accounting. In A the same month would show a loss of $250 while it was actually a profit of $700. Why?

- The #1 item is not reflected in sales on a cash basis because while the work was done and earned it was not collected. However, in the accrual method this is reflected in revenue.
- The #2 item is included in revenue on a cash basis because the cash was received in this month, even though the work was done some other time. This $250 is not included in accrual revenue because the work was not performed in this period.
- #3 was included in both accrual and cash because it was work

both performed in this month and cash collected in this month.

- #4 was $600 paid for six months of insurance. In a cash method that amount would be expensed in the month paid even though it was for many months of insurance. In the accrual system the insurance is allocated as an expense at $100 per month.
- #5 the truck payment of $400 is expensed in the cash system. The accrual system allocates the cost of the truck in the form of depreciation based on the life of the asset and expenses in the current month the interest portion of the payment.

In their own way both systems give the correct answer. But the cash system does not provide data that can be useful in understanding what is going on with the business.

Chapter Three
Accounting Game = Information

To demonstrate some of the things we have covered let's play an accounting card game. Assuming the following facts:

1. Start a new business with an investment of $2,000 cash. The cash is deposited into the company's checking account.
2. Borrow $1,000 from your local banker for the purchase of equipment.
3. You purchase equipment for the business and write a check for $2,000.
4. You make your first sale which is for $2,000 worth of services (which you complete) and then bill the customer who will pay you next month.
5. Your customer sends you a check for $2,000 for work you had done last month.
6. You generate an additional $2,000 in sales for which the customer pays you in cash. You pay business expenses of $1,000.

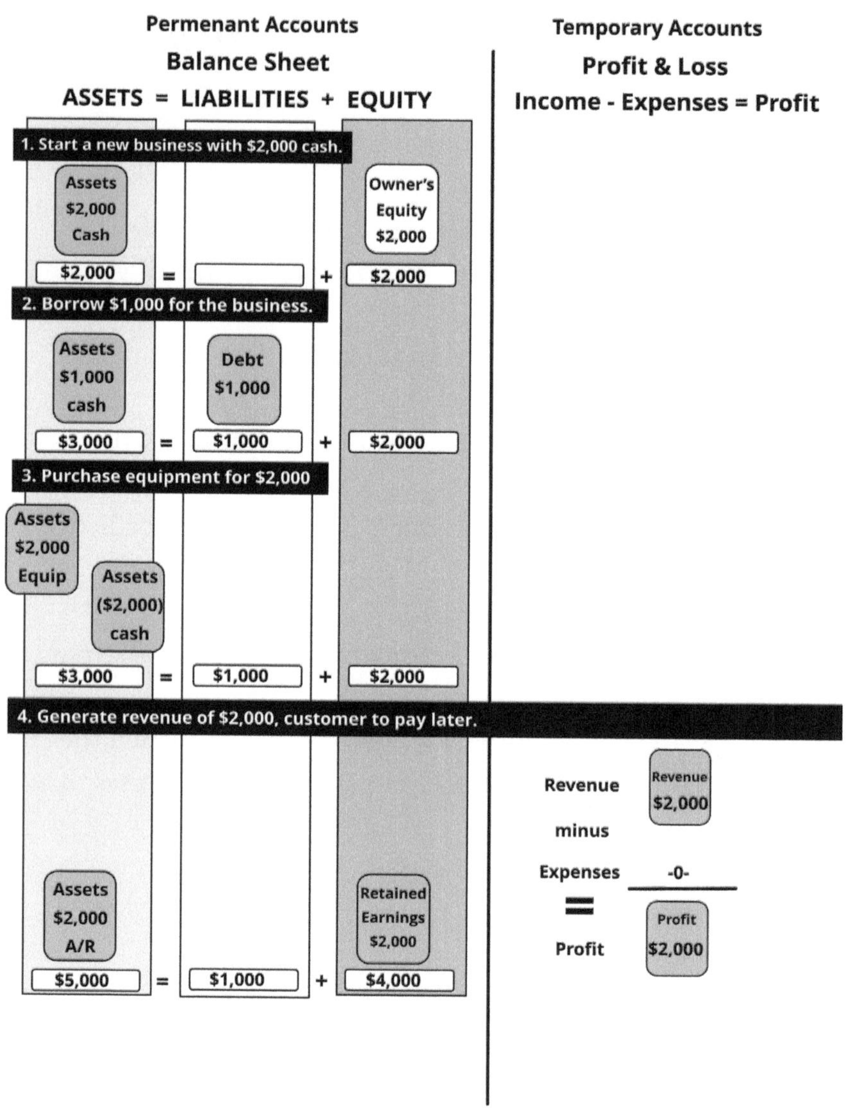
Permenant Accounts
Balance Sheet
ASSETS = LIABILITIES + EQUITY
1. Start a new business with $2,000 cash.
Assets $2,000 Cash
Owner's Equity $2,000
$2,000 = + $2,000
2. Borrow $1,000 for the business.
Assets $1,000 cash
Debt $1,000
$3,000 = $1,000 + $2,000
3. Purchase equipment for $2,000
Assets $2,000 Equip
Assets ($2,000) cash
$3,000 = $1,000 + $2,000
4. Generate revenue of $2,000, customer to pay later.
Assets $2,000 A/R
Retained Earnings $2,000
$5,000 = $1,000 + $4,000
Temporary Accounts
Profit & Loss
Income - Expenses = Profit
Revenue
Revenue $2,000
minus
Expenses -0-
=
Profit
Profit $2,000

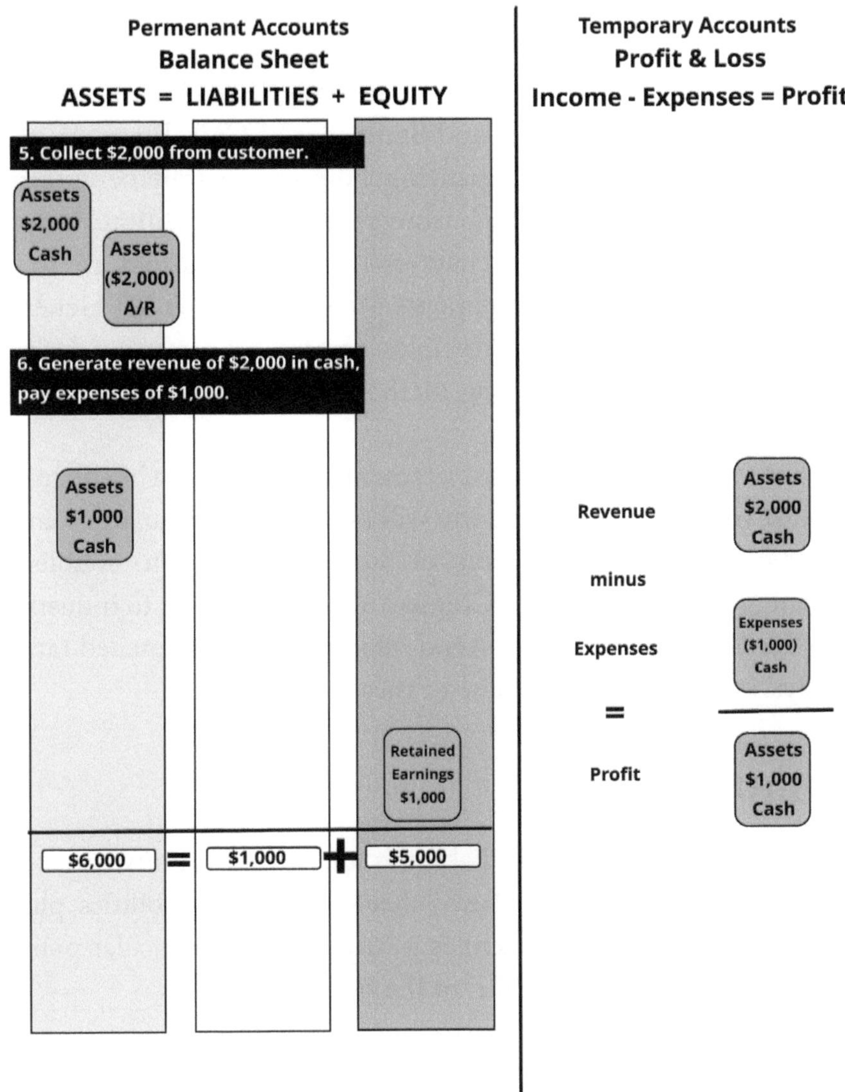
Permenant Accounts
Balance Sheet
ASSETS = LIABILITIES + EQUITY
5. Collect $2,000 from customer.
Assets $2,000 Cash
Assets ($2,000) A/R
6. Generate revenue of $2,000 in cash, pay expenses of $1,000.
Assets $1,000 Cash
Retained Earnings $1,000
$6,000 = $1,000 + $5,000
Temporary Accounts
Profit & Loss
Income - Expenses = Profit
Revenue
Assets $2,000 Cash
minus
Expenses
Expenses ($1,000) Cash
=
Profit
Assets $1,000 Cash

Chapter Four
Financial Statements

The basic financial statements are Income Statement (Profit & Loss, P&L), Balance Sheet and Statement of Cash Flows. With sufficient detail and accompanying notes these statements can tell a complete story about a business's financial condition. As we have discussed in previous chapters there are rules that are followed to produce these statements according to GAAP, Generally Accepted Accounting Principles. Statements can be produced based on different accounting methods, such as cash or another non-GAAP basis.

For a business owner these statements will give you a big picture look at your business. Often you will need additional analysis and comparisons to previous years, or budgets/forecasts to establish meaning to these numbers. Comparing your numbers to industry standards or monitoring for trends along with more detailed ratio analysis will enhance the value of these statements.

Balance Sheet

A balance sheet lists assets, liabilities and owner's equity. The accounting formula for a balance sheet is assets = liabilities plus owner's equity. This statement is a snapshot at a particular point in time of the financial health of the business.

Income Statement

Often called a P&L (Profit & Loss), this statement looks at a period of time. Most typically a P&L is prepared for a one-year cycle, although the business cycle of different industries can be for different periods of time. For that one year cycle the statement is accumulative. At Year-End these temporary accounts reflected on the P&L are closed and the process will start over for the next year. During that one-year period Income Statements are usually prepared on a monthly basis.

The Income Statement reflects revenue, cost or expense accounts and shows either a profit or a loss. Revenue minus costs/ expense equals profit or loss.

To conform to GAAP Income Statements would be prepared on an accrual basis. This often requires extensive adjustments to match revenues and expenses to the proper periods.

Statement of Cash Flows

As the name suggests this is an analysis of activities that impact cash. Debt payments, equipment purchases, and many other activities of a business will not have immediate impact on a P&L but do impact cash. This statement gives the business owner a look at how cash has been used.

Chapter Five
Business Ratios

Financial Statements give you numbers. Those statements can be understood based on standards in your industry, you own businesses past performance, or budgets and goals you have established for your business. Another way to turn those statements into more meaningful data is through ratios.

These ratios are easy to calculate and there is a lot of data available on what they mean, usually related to some industry norm or general business standard. The most important way to use these numbers is to establish your own benchmarks.

Ratios generally fall into three categories:

Liquidity Ratios—these will measure your company's cash or near cash assets in relationship to current liabilities. Are there sufficient liquid assets to meet the short-term needs of the company?

Operating Ratios—these will measure the use of assets and the relationship between assets and financial performance.

Solvency Ratios—these look at the long-term health of the company in relationship of assets and liabilities.

Liquidity Ratios

The **current ratio** measures liquidity in the short term. It is a measure of financial strength. The ratio reflects the number of times current assets exceed current liabilities. Here is the formula to compute the current ratio:

Current Ratio = Total current assets ÷ Total current liabilities

The current ratio is important in that it gives information related to the ability of the business to meet its current obligations. A rule-of-thumb puts a good current ratio at 2 to 1.

The **quick ratio** is also called the acid test ratio. This measure only looks at a company's most liquid assets in relationship to its current liabilities. Here is the formula for the quick ratio:

Quick Ratio = (Current Assets - Inventory) ÷ Current Liabilities

A quick ratio between .50 to 1 is considered to be good.

Operating Ratios

Inventory turnover ratio measures the efficient use of inventory. It is an indication of purchasing and production efficiency. Here is the formula:

Inventory Ratio = Cost of Goods Sold ÷ Inventory
(inventory average for the period measuring)

In general, the higher the turnover the better.

The **sales to receivables ratio** measures the number to times accounts receivables turned over during the period. The higher the turnover of receivables, the shorter the time between sales and when cash is collected. Here is the formula:

Sales to Receivables Ratio = Net Sales ÷ Net Receivables

This is a ratio that you will want to compare to industry standards.

The **days receivables ratio** measures how many days accounts receivable is outstanding. It is computed using the sales/receivables ratio. Here is the formula:

Days Receivables Ratio = 365 ÷ Sales Receivables Ratio

This number only has real meaning as a comparison to industry norms.

A **return on assets ratio** measures the return being generated by the employed assets. It is computed as follows:

Return on Assets = Net Income (Before Taxes) ÷ Total Assets × 100

This is another ratio that only has meaning as a comparison with industry norms.

Solvency Ratios

The **debt to worth ratio** measures the dependence on debt. It is computed as follows:

Debt to Worth Ratio = Total Liabilities ÷ Net Worth

Obviously if this ratio exceeds 1 then more capital is being provided by debt verses owners capital. In itself that might not be bad but can limit a company's ability to borrow additional funds. Generally, bank loan officers will consider a company with a high debt to worth ratio to be of greater risk.

Working capital is more about cash flow than operational performance. Working capital is computed as follows:

Working Capital = Total Current Assets – Total Current Liabilities

Working capital should always be a positive number. Otherwise, the company's obligations would exceed its immediate assets. A company with negative WC would be considered at risk.

The **net sales to working capital** measure is looking at the way working capital is being used. This is also a measure with more meaning as an industry norm than just a standalone number. It is computed as follows:

Net Sales to Working Capital = Net Sales ÷ Net Working Capital

A high ratio means that you may be vulnerable to creditors. This may be dangerous, especially if there is a slowdown in sales.

Chapter Six
Business Structure

Businesses can take the following forms:

- Sole Proprietorship
- Partnership
- Corporation
- S-Corporation
- Limited Liability Company

The simplest form and the one with the fewest reporting requirements, is a sole proprietorship. However, there are good reasons to consider other forms of business structure, some legal, some financial and possibly even just personal preference.

Why Incorporate?

Corporations offer many benefits. For example:

- Personal liability protection.
- Tax advantages.
- Flexibility in structuring pension plans and other owner benefits
- 100% deductibility of health insurance premiums in most cases
- Control in transferring ownership

Protecting Personal Assets.

The number reason to incorporate is the liability protection afforded the creation of a legal entity. While you may own all of the stock of a corporation your personal assets are protected from any action of the corporation that might result in legal action. The downside of this protection is that you must maintain the legal entity's separation and follow all of the requirements in reporting and record keeping and not mix your personal assets with the business assets.

Tax Shelter.

A corporation has special tax rules that apply that are unlike any other entity. Much of this has to do with pensions, profit sharing and stock options that might create favorable advantages when it comes to taxes. Also, health insurance has some special rules for corporations as related to deductibility.

Ownership Structure.

The corporation structure offers advantages related to raising capital, expanding capital, estate planning and many more. Ownership in a corporation can be sold, transferred without dissolving the corporation, which can be a significant advantage in selling the business.

Limited Liability Company

This structure can offer many of the benefits of a corporation and is easier to maintain. A corporation requires board of directors' meetings with minutes and other administrative tasks to maintain the viability of the corporation. Also, a corporation is required to file its own detailed tax return. Most of that is not true for an LLC.

Chapter Seven
Goals, Budgets and Forecasting

If you want to achieve something you need to set a goal to do just that. Business owners should establish goals for themselves and their business. Write it down and measure your advancement towards that goal.

One of the first goals is what do you want to achieve out of the business. Money, fame; well, those are admirable goals but a little on the fuzzy side. When setting goals make them specific. Your business goal might be to sell the business in five years for a billion bucks. Now that is a goal.

The desired outcome of goal setting is to create direct action in achieving the goal. If your business goal is to make a living, your action plan may not be very aggressive. Establish a goal that is achievable but also aggressive enough to prompt positive action to achieve the goal.

I'm a great believer in budgets and forecasting. The difference here is subtle but there is a difference. A budget is setting a detailed goal for your business based on actual expectations. Forecasting is setting goals that are based on do something. A forecast might be what you would expect to happen if you opened ten more stores—it quantifies what-if outcomes.

All goal sitting, budgets and forecasts in one way is guessing. But guessing allows you to see the outcomes that might occur if this or that happen. Also, budgets provide you with a benchmark on what you thought would happen that you can measure actual results against. It's a tool, and you should use it.

Short-term and Long-term Goals

Goals can be for a day, a week, a month or whatever period you want. Short-term goals can be casual—let's agree we are going to do $X in revenue this weekend. This can be team building, getting everyone on the same page. Goals can be long term—here is my ten-year goal. Even though everyone knows we cannot know the future having a mental image of your goal out into the future is a strong motivation to work towards that goal.

Set specific goals and establish timetables to achieve the goal.

Doing better is not a goal. Doing $5,000 in sales next week is. Sales of $5,000 sometime this year is not a goal. It must be specific and cannot be sometime in the future. Set goals with details and specific time frames.

Unachievable Goals are useless.

Our goal for sales today is five billion. Don't set unrealistic goals, you will fail. Sitting goals that are too high or too low is counterproductive. Make your goals aggressive but still achievable.

Meaningful goals.

Goals should move you towards something meaningful and rewarding.

Don't give up on goals setting.

I never achieve these goals; I'm not going to do that anymore. Don't give up, just evaluate what you are doing and set meaningful goals but achievable one. Maybe even toss in an occasional slam dunk, just to keep the enthusiasm going.

Review, review, review.

Monitor your goals often. Don't establish goals and then never measure if you are achieving them. You can revise goals but don't ignore them, otherwise they are useless.

Chapter Eight

Accounting Software

What makes accounting much easier today as the past is computer software. The best example is QuickBooks. I'm not going to recommend any specific program; use should choose what works best for your size of company and expertise in utilizing software; but all my references will be to QuickBooks.

Software options:

- Intuit QuickBooks
- Invoice2go
- Oracle Net Suite
- Zoho Books
- Account Edge Pro
- Sage 50cloud Accounting
- Fresh Books
- Wave Accounting
- Kashoo

The purpose of all these programs is to automate as much as possible the accounting process and provide an easy way to accomplish the complicated task of bookkeeping. I'm sure some work better than others, but those most likely will be personal choices. They all will maintain a set of accounting records.

Often the challenge is not the software but the user. If you are unfamiliar with accounting and how "things" work in that world software can only help so much. To get the maximum benefit from any of this software takes a certain amount of knowledge about the bookkeeping process. Don't expect to just buy the software and everything will work like magic.

One of the first things you do in sitting up the software is establishing a chart of accounts. These accounts are how you classify your business transactions. Most of these programs will allow you to use a "standard" or ready-made set of accounts for your industry. But the more you know the better these initial steps will go.

If you don't know, hire someone who does.

Don't be fooled by the ads or literature that makes it seem like all you must do is install the right software and bookkeeping becomes automatic. It does not work that way. The more you know about accounting the better this software works, and if you know nothing it might be impossible to get it to function. Hire someone to help you. Yes, I said that again, but that is what you should do. Don't guess, you'll just get things messed up.

Now that I've said the software needs expertise to make it work, let me say; most of these programs are amazing. I've used QuickBooks on many small companies but also used this software for very large companies. It is an amazing product and once you understand how to exercise its strengths you will have a very sophisticated accounting system.

Chapter Nine
Accounting Services

If you think accounting is a dirty word, it might be best for you to hire someone to do your accounting. There are numerous bookkeeping firms who will do that for you. You can have someone do your accounting, your payroll, your tax reports, everything can be jobbed out to someone with the expertise to accomplish all these tasks.

The title of this section is easyAccounting. The goal was to show you that accounting is not a mystery, or some magic performed by geeky wizards. It isn't. It is a system that takes data and turns it into something useful such as financial statements or detailed sales reports.

Is it easy? For some, no. I've worked with business owners who ran a successful business but never fully grasped how the numbers came together. Almost all had hired someone to do those tasks and if necessary, explain the numbers. If this is not your thing, don't fight it—hire someone.

One of the worst things I've seen from small businesspeople do is them trying to manage bookkeeping without the skill or knowledge. If you're a great fence builder, then build fences, don't sit in an office, and try to figure out payroll. If you are a genius at fixing gourmet meals, then do it, don't hide in a small office, and try to accomplish producing financial statements.

Make sure you hire the right people, but please don't try to become a bookkeeper just because you don't want to admit you have no interest in learning accounting. Learn how to use accounting information but don't try to be the bookkeeper, it will be an unpleasant experience and sour you on the whole process of what accounting is all about.

Okay, so the title is a lie; there is no easyAccounting. But there is a better way of understanding what accounting is trying to accomplish and realize how important it is to your business success, easy or not.

Chapter Ten
Accounting Structure

To have good records you will need an accounting structure for your business. This is the process that records sales, tracks expense, keeps paper records when required, that monitors payroll data and employee records. It also involves monitoring how items are used, stored, counted, expensed. It establishes are revenue is recorded, how it is measured, how it is billed to the customer. The accounting structure is everything to do with numbers and is vital to have a good financial reporting system.

Generally, business transaction has some kind of document that supports that transaction, and the handling of that document is the basis of the accounting structure. But, of course, that is not always true. You can have transactions that are not supported by a document, and you will need to establish how those are handled and what information needs to be gathered.

You can purchase the best computer system, most expensive accounting software and hired an experienced bookkeeper and if all of your support structure is generating garbage your accounting reports will be useless.

This is another area where you may need help. Hire an accountant or bookkeeper and have them review how you are creating and collecting data within your business. The proper creation of these support documents will determine the accuracy of your accounting data.

Every business type or industry will have various ways to handle all of the paperwork so that accounting records are reliable. Don't re-invent the wheel. Ask trade associations or groups if they have anything available on how to structure the paper flow in your type of business. Find an accountant who has a background in your industry can also be helpful.

Also never stop improving this structure. If something is going wrong fix it. If data is not dependable find out where the holes are and plug them. Always be monitoring on how things are done in your business. Don't just assume that it is working correctly. Bad data will lead to bad decisions. It is your job as owner to make sure all of the parts of the accounting structure are in place to provide you with reliable and accurate data so that you decision making is based on facts not guesswork.

I know I'm repeating myself but if you need to, hire someone to help. You might think you can afford to spend that money on an accountant, but without good data you are flying blind, and your chances of success are lessened. Now can you make your fortune without accounting, sure; but it is harder. Why not get this numbers stuff right at the beginning and use good information to make good business decisions?

Good Luck!

Conclusion

Why isn't accounting easy? Part of this is because accounting is based on a set of rules that are not intuitive and in most cases aren't even known by many people trying to understand accounting. It's hard to follow the rules if you don't know them.

Bookkeeping has been a basic of business for a long, long time. I think bookkeeping had a different feel when they were actual books. Now the computer does stuff and out pops some financial statement. While that may appear to be magic it is not. The results are complete garbage if what was put in was garbage.

As a businessperson you are responsible to create the right accounting structure so that your accounting system will produce useful, accurate reporting. Without that accurate reporting you are flying blind in a snowstorm. You need data to manage a business to success.

Spending money on an accounting system, or accounting expertise to help you structure the accounting workflow is an investment in the future of your business.

Most small business owners are hands-on managers who value the knowledge they gain working within the business, but even with that hands-on approach you will need financial data to be able to maximize the chances of achieving success. It can be done without good accounting, but it is harder and more difficult to duplicate.

Never be afraid of admitting that accounting is not your strength, which is the smart thing to do; now hire someone to help you build this tool that will improve all of your other management skills and increase the odds of you achieving success in your business venture.

Today there are POS systems, industry specific workflow

systems, industry specific accounting software and an army of qualified professionals to assist in this area. There is no excuse not to have good financial and operational data to enhance your management decisions.

Big business has an edge when it comes to operational data, but you have an edge as a small business owner because of you and your commitment. Don't let this weakness in good data blunt that edge and keep you from achieving your dreams.

Stay in Touch

Stay in touch with Ted Clifton and Success Paths business books. Clifton's background is financial (CPA, Controller, CFO) with over 30 years of real-world experience as a financial advisor, business owner of fifteen business ventures and as a business broker with valuation experience.

Learn more about successful business practices and small business matters, such as selling or buying a business, starting and running a small business and how to value a small business.

Newsletters are free and informative. Opt-out at any time. Thanks for your interest in Success Paths Business Books.

Subscribe today at:
https://mailchi.mp/1e966d569a72/success-paths

Ted Clifton Mystery Books

Business books and mystery books might be an odd combination, but maybe they are connected in a mysterious way—if you enjoy mysteries, check out these offerings from Ted Clifton. Learn more at www.tedclifton.com.

Pacheco & Chino Mysteries—A retired sheriff, an enigmatic bait-shop owner, and an Apache fishing guide team up to solve a mystery that starts with an out-of-place show dog—and ends much deadlier.

The Bootlegger's Legacy—Joe and Mike, middle-aged losers, have uncovered a promise of abundant riches—if only they can solve the clues left behind by Mike's bootlegger dad.

Vincent Malone—Disgraced investigator and alcoholic Vincent Malone finds new life as a shuttle driver for a B&B—then a guest is murdered and his investigative skills are suddenly front-and-centre again.

The Muckraker Series—New journalism grad Tommy Jacks hires on as a political reporter with a struggling paper, but is quickly pulled into an ugly newspaper war when a rival reporter is murdered.

Doctor Hightower—Ted Clifton's new Mystery/Sci-Fi serial, available on Amazon Vella soon!

Ted Clifton Series Starter Set—Amazon ebook containing the complete first books of the Pacheco & Chino, Vincent Malone, and Muckraker mystery series.

Have questions or comments for Ted Clifton? He can be reached at ask@tedclifton.com.

Thanks for being a reader!

www.ingramcontent.com/pod-product-compliance
Ingram Content Group UK Ltd.
Pitfield, Milton Keynes, MK11 3LW, UK
UKHW041640190726
13854UKWH00006B/2613